TIDBITS
THE BOOK II

**All The News You Never Knew
That You Never Needed To Know®**

Published By
Steele Media, Inc.
Billings, Montana

Tidbits® The Book II

is published by
Steele Media, Inc.
P.O. Box 1255
Billings, MT 59103
(406) 248-9000

The authors have gathered information in <u>Tidbits®</u> <u>The</u> <u>Book</u> <u>II</u> from sources considered to be reliable; however, the accuracy of all information cannot be guaranteed.

You may obtain additional copies of this book from Steele Media, Inc., or directly from your local publisher of the Tidbits® paper.

Cover Design: Rob Johnson, Mission Graphics

Illustrator: Steve Hogan

Lithography: ABBAgraphics, Inc.

ISBN 0-9663571-1-6

Printed in the United States of America

Dedicated to:

Tidbits® Publishers
across the United States

Without you, this book would not be possible.

– David L. and Cecelia Steele

ACKNOWLEDGEMENTS

This book is possible because of the hard work and dedication of many key people who believe in Tidbits®. We are grateful to our free-lance writers Valmarie Darrington, Mona Lee McKown, Janice C. Walker and Kathy Wolfe and appreciate their hard work and dedication in finding obscure and interesting pieces of information. We want to thank our illustrator Steve Hogan and proofreader Dru Wagner. Many thanks to Holli Prociv, our free-lance desktop publisher and editor, who compiled this information into its present format. Last but not least, we are grateful to Tidbits® paper publishers across the country and to all their advertisers and readers. These are the real Tidbits® heros.

INTRODUCTION

A tidbit is defined as, *"a morsel of food to be devoured before the meal."* That's what Tidbits® is ...food for thought. The Tidbits® paper is a weekly entertainment newspaper, devoted to publishing things you didn't know and distributed almost exclusively in restaurants. The Tidbits® paper is published by more than 100 independent publishers across the country. <u>Tidbits</u>® <u>The</u> <u>Book</u> <u>II</u> is a compilation of 26 Tidbits® issues that were previously published in the Tidbits® paper.

Bon Appetit!

CONTENTS

1

THE LAW

By J.C. Walker

Quick Quote

- "Good laws lead to the making of better ones; bad ones bring about worse. As soon as any man says of the affairs of the State, 'What does it matter to me?' the State may be given up for lost."   *– Jean Jacques Rousseau*

Just the Facts, Ma'am

- Our word *justice* comes from the Emperor of Byzantine who lived from 482 to 565, Justinian. He codified the loose collection of Roman laws then in use, and many legal maxims today are derived from Justinian's books.

Who Loves Ya, Shlomo

- They say you can get anything you want in New York City 24 hours a day, but you can't get this on Saturday. The headturner at the Rockland County Police Academy is Shlomo Koenig, the first Hasidic cop in history. The Orthodox Jew, who wears the proscribed curly sidelocks, traditional bowler hat and long coat while at his plastic-shopping-bag factory, was asked by a local sheriff to apply for training at the academy as a way to educate local police forces about the cultural differences and prohibitions of the rapidly expanding Orthodox and ultra-conservative Jewish sects in the Brooklyn area. While the sidelocks are not the look associated with the Smokey the Bear hat and aviator glasses of the typical law-enforcer, Shlomo offers valuable assistance to a population that often doesn't speak English, watch television, drive cars on the Sabbath, or mingle between the

2

sexes. There is also a history of oppression by police forces in Eastern Europe which forced many Orthodox Jews to emigrate to the U.S. at the end of the last century. Shlomo's presence as a police officer in the neighborhoods quells many of those old fears. "I'm a Jew first, a police officer second," he says. "I still try to live on my own in my smaller world. I try to do my studying, my praying, the religious education of my kids. I also try to be a sheriff. I have to be able to work with society, and I try to do that."

Good News, Bad News Department

- The good news for Anthony Colclasure of Fairfield, Illinois, was that he won $1,000 in the state lottery. The bad news was that he was notified of his winnings while sitting in the Wayne County Jail. The good news was that Anthony would receive $870 after paying taxes on his winnings. The bad news was that his bail was $400. The good news was that he could mail in the ticket to the lottery claims office to collect. The bad news was that he couldn't get out of jail to cash the check.

Death by Couture

- One of the least known lawmakers in history was a Greek attorney named Draco. Even though he lived more than 2500 years ago, his influence is still felt in a variety of ways today. He was one of the first in history to define and write down a specific code for punishments to be meted out by the state, rather than rely on the consequences of family retaliation to secure justice. While the idea that a crime was an offense against the state, rather than an individual, was commendable, Draco went just a wee bit overboard in his penalities—usually death in some gruesome manner for even the most trivial of transgressions. That's why we use the word *draconian* to describe an especially harsh law or judgement. The greatest irony of the lawmaker's life, however, was the manner in which he died: Draco was adored to death by the citizenry of Athens. When an adored person entered an auditorium, he would be showered with the hats and cloaks of enthusiastic supporters. Draco, the lawmaker who meted out the cruelest of punishments, was smothered to death by the huge pile of garments thrown by his fans in a show of overwhelming civility.

License to Fail

- A 73-year-old man in Buinerveen, Netherlands, was recently cited for driving without a license. He says if he doesn't pass the test, he won't try again. This is great, except the man had been driving without a license for more than 30 years, and after the citation he flunked the driving test 17 times. Fortunately for him, the Dutch have a special type of car called an "invalid auto" which doesn't require a standard driver's license. Fortunately for the rest of us, the vehicle can reach speeds of only 45 kilometers (28 mph).

So Sue Me

- Another great lawmaker in history was Alfred the Great of England, who ruled in the late 9th century. Like Draco, he saw the necessity for making crimes a travesty against the king, rather than an individual, and in that way he was able to end the cycle of blood feuds between families. He decided to "gather the old laws of the Saxons together and commanded many of those to be written which our forefathers held, those which to me seem good" as the first sort of legal reform. This was a considerable improvement over the arbitrary and often corrupt justice doled out by local officials. He also called upon the legal boundaries defined by the Ten Commandments, although he didn't go as far as Draco in determining punishments. Alfred is probably also considered a patron saint by many people in the legal professions—he was the first lawmaker to decide that monetary compensation was reasonable in bodily injury cases. He decided, for example, that a wound one inch long was worth a shilling, a broken tooth six shillings, and a severed ear would get a plaintiff 20 shillings.

The Woman Behind the Badge

- The National Sheriff's Association estimates there were 19 women sheriffs as of 1995, and the new sheriff, Delena Goss, of Tahlequah, Oklahoma, has her work cut out for her. In the novel about the town, *Zeke and Ned*, authors Larry McMurtry and Diana Ossana describe it as "a place so wild that the law had no chance of prevailing." Goss campaigned with the motto, "Time for a Change," which wasn't surprising, given that her predecessor and staff were being charged with sexual battery on a dispatcher, failure to control evidence and employees, misuse of time by playing games with prisoners, prejudicial treatment, allowing use of county equipment for personal gain, improper use of firearms, and grand larceny. Goss has instituted a no-smoking policy in the department and has rescinded the practice of handing out "honorary deputy cards" to special friends. Morale has picked up considerably in the department since she arrived. The only problem she's had upon taking office is equipment—she was immediately issued a gun, a pager and a cellular phone, but her badge took months to arrive. In the meantime, she wore a small gold angel pinned to the lapel of her jacket.

Legal Eagle

- King Edward I ruled England in the late 1200s and set the stage for many legal matters we take for granted today. He regularly summoned public assemblies to decide state and legal issues, and he also organized a police system to preserve the peace. The news wasn't all good, though—he also invented the legal profession by developing a certification procedure for "those so chosen should follow the Court and take part in its business and no others."

Pretty in Pink

- The jail in Davidson County, North Carolina, is not a pretty place. Inmates are not served coffee, nor are they allowed television or cigarettes. They wear black and white striped uniforms and work eight hours a day cleaning up highways, swamps, and church graveyards. Sheriff Gerald Hege also extends their punishment to jail decor as well. Although he says he got the idea for the color scheme while visiting the Grand Canyon during a beautiful sunset, he admits "after three or four days, it does get to you." What is this cruel and unusual decorating motif? Hege had the entire jail interior painted in Pepto Bismol pink, embellished with large blue teddy bears crying white tears. Inmates for the most part have not been supportive, he reports. "There's kind of a humiliating aspect to it. It's hard to be macho in a pink cell with blue teddy bears."

Enough with the Post Mortems

- Jeremy Bentham was a famous legal reformer in England in the early 1800s. His presence is still felt today in more ways than one. Although he never actually practiced law, he was responsible for getting the death penalty revoked for many minor infractions against the King. He was also hugely popular with the people throughout Europe, and France even made him an honorary citizen in 1792. He was so popular, in fact, that when he died in 1832, his head was cut off, his body embalmed, and a wax copy of his head attached. The body still lies in state at University College in London.

The Law Hall of Shame

- Two Cochise County, Arizona, sheriff's deputies couldn't believe their eyes when they looked in the back of a pickup truck they'd stopped for a minor traffic infraction. Sitting in plain view were 193 pounds of marijuana, neatly baled, stacked and ready for distribution.

Wired

- Figuring child support payments, taking a case to small claims court, filing for divorce, or disputing your landlord's eviction are stressful enough, but the stress and inconvenience are only worsened by trips to governmental offices and long waits in line. Officials in Arizona think they've found a way to alleviate a lot of bureaucratic hassles, though—they've set up electronic kiosks, like ATMs, in convenient areas where people can electronically fill in documents with the machine's help. Oddly, it was so popular that appointments had to be made to use the machines—150 systems at new locations were added.

Follow That Byte

- As if the Internet hasn't taken over our lives enough, a recent arraignment in New York City brought to light a whole new cyber-ruse: electronic ambulance chasing. Eight lawyers, two doctors, three emergency medical workers and four people identified as "chasers" were recently charged with finding victims of accidents who were immediately referred to injury lawyers on-line. Often the victims received solicitation phone calls within minutes of their injuries. One of the attorneys had sent notices out by e-mail that said: "I run a consulting firm that specializes in injuries covered by no-fault and workers' compensation. I have a network of hospital workers and paramedics that refer cases to me and would like to extend an offer to you ... $200 per eligible referral." Police report the numbers were more like "$300 for referring someone with a soft tissue injury, and as much as $1,000 for someone with a fracture."

I Fought the Law and the Law Won

- It was a high-speed three-mile chase through the busiest sections of downtown Florence, Alabama, and the escapee died at the scene, but no charges of police brutality are being leveled against the officers. A bull ran out of a sale barn outside of town and caused quite a commotion when he charged Animal Control staff, jumped up and kicked in the grill of their truck, and charged away to what appeared to be a clean getaway. Unfortunately for the bull, the officers carefully approached what they thought was a resting animal and found that he had instead keeled over and died. The critter could not be revived in spite of the Animal Control staff's efforts to bring him back with mouth-to-mouth resuscitation.

License to Steal

- A pair of robbers in Kentucky get an "E" for Effort but an "F" for Follow-through. They hit on the bright idea of chaining the bumper of their truck to the front of an after-hours ATM machine, thinking this would pull it off and make the loot inside readily available. They lost their cool, though, when it was the machine that pulled the bumper off the truck instead, and they drove away in a panic. Unfortunately for them, they forgot that the license plate on the truck was also attached to the bumper. It took police all of about 15 minutes to figure out who the thieves were and to arrest them.

Let Your Fingers Do the Walking

- In Arizona, a company called "Guns for Hire" provides actors for Western movie scripts and amusement parks, and it advertises prominently in the phone book. Apparently, this specialty is not always entirely clear to potential clients, as a woman recently was sentenced to 4 years in jail when she called the casting office and said she wished to use their services to kill her husband.

Pretty as a Picture

- It wasn't very hard to find the robber of a Dallas bank recently. In addition to helping himself to the loot in an after-hours heist, the thief thought he'd also make a few extra bucks selling the video surveillance camera mounted by the door. What he overlooked was that, as he was disconnecting the camera, he was constantly being photographed, and his image was being recorded on a videotape in another part of the building.

2

IN YOUR CUPBOARDS
by Kathy Wolfe

In the Kitchen

- A popular 1830s housekeeping manual stated, "The home in which the kitchen is neglected is not a healthy or a happy home."
- It takes 10 pounds of milk to make 1 pound of natural cheese. Milk is 87% water. During the process of making cheese, the water is separated and removed. This is called the whey, and accounts for about 9 out of the 10 pounds of milk. The remainder is the curd, which is what becomes the cheese.
- The fruit flavorings used in Wrigleys Juicy Fruit gum are lemon, orange, pineapple, and banana.
- Yogurt is richer in calcium than milk is; in fact, almost one times more. Research has also shown that consistent yogurt eaters have a lower risk of colon cancer.
- It takes more than 1,200 peanuts to make a 28-ounce jar of peanut butter. By the time a person graduates from high school, he has already eaten 1,500 peanut butter and jelly sandwiches.
- An Armenian immigrant, P. P. Halajian, and five of his fellow Armenians invested $6,000 in 1919 to open a candy business which featured coconut dipped in chocolate. Since Mr. Halajian's name was Peter Paul, this was the name chosen for the company that marketed Mounds bars.
- Henry Perky rolled softened wheat berries into airy little biscuits in 1892, thus creating the first version of Shredded Wheat cereal.

- The first "prize" in a cereal box was a paper airplane cutout in 1943.
- 700,000 acres of forest are owned by Kimberly-Clark, the Kleenex and paper towel giants.
- "A little dab'll do ya." No, not Brylcreem, but Tabasco sauce on your gums to relieve a toothache.
- "I love hot sauce. I splash Tabasco all over." – *George Bush*

On The Shelf

- Bees have to visit two million flowers to make one pound of honey. The worker bee spends its entire lifetime buzzing from one blossom to the next, only to yield one-twelfth of one teaspoon for a life's worth of labors. And that buzzing sound you hear is the 11,400 flaps of its wings every minute.
- S.O.S. pads have been around since 1913. It was the inventor's wife who dubbed the steel wool pads S.O.S., which stands for "Save Our Saucepans."
- Contrary to popular belief, the potato is not fattening. A medium-sized boiled potato contains about 100 calories, fewer calories than an apple has.
- Earl Silas Tupper was an employee of the DuPont chemical company when he began experimenting with plastic. He developed containers with airtight seals, using a paint can with its flared rim and locking lid as a model. It's estimated that Earl's new products, Tupperware, can now be found in 90% of America's cupboards.
- The first town to manufacture a certain famous little fig cookie was Newton, Massachusetts; hence, the name Fig Newtons.

In The Bathroom

- Shampoo was first marketed in the U.S. in 1930 by John Breck, who was the captain of a volunteer fire department in Massachusetts.
- Coca-Cola can be used to clean stains from your toilet bowl. Let it sit for an hour before brushing. The name Coca-Cola, which was trademarked in 1893, comes from two of the beverage's main ingredients, the coca leaf and the kola nut.

The inventor of Coke also patented Indian Queen Hair Dye and Triplex Liver Pills.

- Denture cleanser is also an effective toilet bowl cleaner, as well as a great diamond cleaner.
- A CIA agent has revealed that this government agency has used poisonous toothpaste as a method of assassination.
- It was "Ted Mack's Amateur Hour" that helped boost the sales of Geritol for iron-poor, tired blood. Its claim to fame was that it was rich with "twice the iron in a pound of calf's liver." The product name is a blend of "geriatric" (meaning "old age") and "tolerance."
- The name "Vaseline" is a combination of the German word for "water"—*wasser.* The Greek word for "olive oil" is *elaion.*

On The Dressing Table

- The Band-Aid came along in the early 1920s when the uncoordinated wife of a young Johnson & Johnson employee regularly cut herself while performing household duties. Her husband always tended to her wounds, but grew tired of the gauze bandages falling off. The self-adhesive Band-Aid was the result.
- The inventor of Ivory Soap, Harley Procter, took the name out of the Bible from Psalm 45, which speaks of "ivory palaces." Harley's cousin was a chemist named James Gamble, who helped him develop his formula, and the partnership of Procter and Gamble was born. Ivory's famous trademark of floatability occurred by accident when an employee neglected to shut off the mixing machine, causing too much air to be whipped into the batch. Customers love its ability to float, but might not realize that all that whipped air causes Ivory to dissolve nearly twice as quickly as other soaps.
- Max Factor was a wigmaker in Russia until the age of 27 when he visited America with the sole purpose of setting up a booth at the 1904 St. Louis World's Fair. He decided to stay, opening a perfume, makeup, and wig shop in St. Louis. Factor's ambition led him to Hollywood where his

famous clients launched his company into the lead in the cosmetics business.

- In 1923, Leo Gerstenzag's wife was cleaning her baby's ears with a piece of cotton on the end of a toothpick. This inspired Leo to invent the Q-Tip.

- T.L. Williams founded the Maybelline Company in 1915, naming his new business after his sister, Mabel.

- Lemon juice is said to relieve the itching caused by poison ivy.

- If you run out of shaving cream, either peanut butter or olive oil are suitable substitutes.

- The Colgate Company, which introduced Colgate Dental Cream in 1896, was originally in the business of making starch, soap, and candles.

- If you love what Alka-Seltzer does for your upset stomach, but can't stand the taste of it, try putting a teaspoon of vanilla extract in the glass.

- It is not a good idea to use sunscreen that is more than a year old, as its sun protection ability is diminished.

All Through The House

- Turtle Wax received its name from a stream called Turtle Creek. It seems the inventor of the car polish was relaxing briefly in this peaceful spot while on a road trip when the idea hit him that his product was "tough as a turtle shell." "Plastone Liquid Car Polish" became "Turtle Wax."

- The yo-yo was first patented in the U.S. in 1929.

- The ball-point pen has been around only since 1945. It was such a novelty, it sold for $12.50. Ten years later, Frenchman Marcel Bich was selling his disposable ball-point for about 19 cents, with sales of two million per week in France alone.

He dropped the "h" from his surname for simplicity, and gained fame with his Bic pens.

- Yes, there was a Milton Bradley. One of his pre-board-game places of employment was with a printer, who was hired to print hundreds of thousands of campaign photographs of the Republican candidate in the 1860 presidential election—Abraham Lincoln. The first board game he sold was LIFE, which he bought from another inventor shortly after the Civil War.

- "A rapidly revolving brush loosens the dust which is sucked back into the dirt bag." – *the first ad for Hoover vacuum cleaners, manufactured by the Electric Suction Sweeper Company, 1908.*

- Herman Fisher and Irving Price joined up in the toy business in 1930, constructing all their toys from Ponderosa pine. Sales were $116,000 for 1932 and $400,000,000 in 1990.

- Frederick Maytag was a buggy maker before breaking into the washing machine business in 1909. In addition to his "gyrofoam washer" manufacturing, he served as mayor of Newton, Iowa, and served two terms in the State Senate.

- Crayons were first made in 1903 and sold for a nickel for eight colors. The wife of the creator dubbed them Crayola by combining the French word for "chalk"—*craie*—with "ola" from the word *oleanginous*, which means "oily." By the time your child is 10, he or she will have worn down about 730 crayons.

The Stuff In Your Cupboard

- That bottle of Worcestershire Sauce in your cupboard contains ingredients that were stirred together two years before they were bottled. Some of these include vinegar, molasses, garlic, and tamarinds (tropical fruits with an acidic pulp).

- Eight million miles of aluminum foil are used in the homes of America each year.

- Saran Wrap has been around since 1953. Zip-Loc bags entered the market in 1970.

- Arthur Meyerhoff was co-founder of the company who first

marketed a non-sticking cooking spray. Arthur's daughter's name was Pam, whose name now adorns the millions of cans sold annually.

- It takes a coffee tree until it is six to eight years old to bear fruit. After that, it produces enough fruit to produce about one pound of coffee annually. Instant coffee is made by brewing coffee in large containers, then evaporating all the liquid. The largest producer of coffee is Brazil, with 30% of the world's crop.
- Although the United States consumes about 2,600,000,000 pounds of coffee every year, tea is still the world's most popular beverage. Scotsman Sir Thomas Lipton introduced his famous brand in America in 1888.
- The world's largest food company is the Nestl Company, and their biggest seller is the Kit-Kat bar, with more than 350 Kit-Kat "fingers" consumed every second through the world. Nestl also owns Carnation, Ortega, and Friskies, to mention a few.

The Wonder Liquid And More

- Use that bottle of club soda to clean your diamonds, remove grease from knit fabrics, eradicate wine stains from the carpet, and to relieve indigestion.
- Philadelphia Brand cream cheese has never been manufactured in that city. Its creator, J.L. Kraft, gave it that name merely because Philadelphia was home to many high-quality food companies in 1882, the year it was first made, in New York City.
- It was at the 1904 St. Louis World's Fair that the nation first put yellow mustard on its hot dogs. It was the brainstorm of two brothers, George and Francis French, who sold their mustard company 22 years later for $4 million.
- Daniel Dole traveled to Hawaii to visit family, who had been missionaries there. While there, he invested his entire life savings in an industry he knew absolutely nothing about—pineapple. His gamble took a few years, but the 75,000

pineapple plants he planted on 12 acres eventually paid off. He also developed a peeling and coring machine.

- Italian immigrant Hector Boiardi operated a small restaurant in Cleveland. His customers loved his recipes so much, he began selling his tomato sauce in bottles to patrons. He then began selling his cheeses, and finally sold entire ready-to-prepare dinners from the counter in his restaurant. He later marketed these dinners under the name Chef Boyardee, an easier pronunciation of his Italian name.

- Isaac Singer ran away from home at age 12 to become a traveling actor, his profession for the next 12 years. Being a mechanical sort, he then set to work on perfecting an improved sewing machine, for which he received a patent in 1851. His personal life perhaps kept him from greater financial success—it was discovered he was the father of 24 children by four different women.

- WD-40 received its name from its Water Displacement formula and the fact that its inventor finally reached success with his formula on the 40th attempt.

- Approximately 70% of American homes have an answering machine.

- Kingsford charcoal briquets were developed by Henry Ford. He was looking for a use for the huge piles of wood scraps generated by his Model T factory, and used a process to turn these scraps into charcoal. When one of his relatives, E.G. Kingsford, came up with a site for the charcoal factory, Henry Ford gave the former Ford Charcoal Company a new name.

- Elmer's Glue was originally known as "Cascorez" and was found on grocery store shelves in a 2-ounce glass jar with a wooden applicator.

- Vanilla was first imported to the United States by Thomas Jefferson, who tasted it on a journey to France.

- The Michelin Rubber Company was founded in 1830, but didn't enter the tire-making business until 1891 when the air-inflated tire was developed.

Contain a Grain of Truth

- In ancient Assyria the famous Greek physician Galen suggested applying a paste of powdered bees and honey on the scalp to restore hair. Pearls dissolved in lemon juice once were recommended by European herbalists as a treatment for epilepsy. In the 17th century, placing green walnuts in the ear was considered a cure for deafness.

- While specific food legends may be pure entertainment, modern science is showing that many historically popular foods are indeed good for you and should be part of a healthy diet.

- Walnuts were part of our ancestors' diet as far back as 7000 BC. They are a good source of protein and fiber as well as vitamins, like B6 and thiamin, and minerals, like copper and magnesium. They also contain essential fatty acids that the body cannot make on its own. Walnuts are one of the best non-fish sources of important omega-3 fatty acids that help protect the heart.

- It's important to remember that not all fat is bad. The kind to avoid is saturated fat, the kind found in animal products. Unsaturated fats, like monounsaturated and polyunsaturated, the kind found in walnuts, provide vital protection against certain diseases.

- Recent studies have shown that walnuts can reduce your risk of heart disease and stroke. A study at Loma Linda University published in the New England Journal of Medicine in 1993 showed that walnuts can reduce your total and "bad" cholesterol, thus reducing your coronary risk. And another study at University of California at San Francisco published in Stroke, the journal of the American Heart Association, in 1995 suggested that linolenic acid, which is found in walnuts, can help prevent blood clotting and arrhythmia that causes strokes.

- It's easy to get the nutritious benefits of walnuts. Just sprinkle them on salads, fruit, cereals, vegetables, rice and pasta to add wonderful taste and texture.

3

TRUTH IS STRANGER THAN FICTION

By J.C. Walker

No Bilge

- During World War II, a gymnasium hundreds of miles from the ocean was commissioned by the United States Navy. Bear Down Gym at the University of Arizona in Tucson was pulled out of service as the site for the school's basketball games, its floors were covered with masonite, and 500 bunk beds were installed to house Navy personnel for the duration. The facility was named U.S.S. Bear Down, making it the only building in U.S. history to have served in active duty during wartime as a ship.

Fantasy

- A recent survey revealed who receives the most fan mail in the world. It's not a popular singer or politician or anyone who even has an actual fan club—the two people in the world with the biggest mailboxes are Pope John Paul II and Mother Teresa. Not only do they receive thousands of letters every day, but also countless wedding invitations, birth, and death announcements.

- Country singer Dolly Parton recently disbanded her fan club and sent back outstanding annual dues which were to be used to fund the Dollywood Foundation projects. Saying that it bothered her to profit from her fans' devotion, she admitted she "knew people were donating because of their personal feelings, and not because they wanted to contribute to the charitable foundation."

Not Above the Law

- Police Sgt. Steven Rogers of Nutley, New Jersey, recently received an urgent call while having lunch at a local diner. The complaint was about illegal parking, which happened to be his squad car. He promptly wrote himself a ticket for $17 and moved on.

Bulletin

- A heavily mined island deep in the middle of the Korean demilitarized zone was the unlikely location of a recent multinational humanitarian project—no bull. Seems a bull had floated downstream in heavy flooding last summer and found himself stranded on Yoo-Do Island which lies in no-man's land between North and South Korea. A rescue plan was soon developed by the U.N. Command officers and forwarded to the South Koreans. They replied they thought the starving bull was doing fine, that they would drop feed on the island to help out, and that maybe North Korea could contribute to his rehabilitation by thoughtfully leaving a cow on the island. This alternative was not a hit with local environmentalists, who pointed out that the island was, after all, loaded with land mines and that the non-native grazing animals and their progeny would destroy natural vegetation and endanger rare birds. All sides agreed to forgo military procedure as the animal was lifted off the island by helicopter.

Your Money or Your Mercedes

- Fundraisers in Berkeley, California, came up with a novel way to make money for charity during the holiday season last year. Unabashedly using liberal guilt as a powerful weapon for the poor, the group put fake parking tickets under the wiper blades of luxury cars. The Berkeley Ecumenical Chaplaincy targeted Mercedes, Lexus, Lincoln and BMW owners with official-looking documents that asked them to join Drivers for Dignity with a $300 donation. That sum was chosen because it's the typical monthly payment for such a vehicle, and, as the group stated, "One $300 donation will pay housing costs for one person to participate in the program for a month."

Stop Me Before I Eat Again

- A thief in West Palm Beach, Florida, was recently sentenced to six years in prison for stealing $30,000 in jewels in 1995. Apparently, the defense he whipped up didn't convince the jury—he claimed he had been an undiagnosed diabetic before the heist and that the two bags of cotton candy he ate triggered uncharacteristic larcenous behavior.

Don't Drop and Drive

- At Times Square in New York City they mark the passage of the New Year with the dropping of a huge illuminated ball. Not to be outdone, the townspeople of Falmouth, Pennsylvania, are preparing the 6th annual Falmouth goat-lowering ceremony. The event, attended by as many as 500 people, was originally conceived as homage to the festivities in October that center on the town's goat run. At this event are goat races, a craft show, tractor pull and chicken-flying contest. Similar activities, with seasonal variations, are also held on New Year's, accompanied by bingo, Karaoke, and a toy rocket contest for kids. Rockets are judged by their appearance, and then blasted off at midnight during the goat drop. Lest animal rights activists be concerned, the goat is constructed of pipe, cloth, and Styrofoam horns.

Big Gulp

- Now that's romance. A happy couple in Richmond, Virginia, recently said their wedding vows at the spot where they met late one fateful night last year—the checkout counter at the nearby 7-Eleven. The bride-to-be was working the late shift when the man of her

Where Else Can You Get Married And Get 3 Hot Dogs For A Buck dreams dropped by for a cup of coffee. Their eyes met over the Big Bite hot dogs, and the rest is history. The store didn't close down during the ceremony, which confused a few customers when the formally gowned bride walked down the baby food and snack chip aisle, but even uninvited guests commented that it was a beautiful wedding. Catering was no problem, either, as the reception line was held next to the beef jerky display.

What a Tangled Web We Weave

- Sometimes, we think computer nerds might be taking this whole virtual reality thing much too far—like too heavy on the virtual and too light on the reality. A recent cruise through the Net uncovered a site where budding entrepreneurs were setting up business for small companies to advertise on the Net within their Website. When it came time to promote it, however, they got a little carried away with the reality part. Calling the site "CyberTowers," the promoters advertised online offices with a selection of office locations—standard deluxe, executive, or professional suites—and decorator samples of wallpaper and color options to suit the "tenants'" tastes.

Special Today

- Telemarketers in Oklahoma City couldn't complain about a slow day earlier this year. Sueanna Jones was selling carpet and vent cleaning when her phone call to Marguerite Vincint took on a more urgent message than carpet mites—Mrs. Vincent began gasping for breath and slurring her words. Thinking quickly, Sueanna yelled to her supervisor that the potential client was having some sort of attack, and an ambulance was called immediately. Mrs. Vincent is recovering nicely at her sister's home, and the telemarketing team on duty that day has "adopted" her as their surrogate grandmother.

Solid Evidence

- Researchers recently reported the findings of a hard-hitting investigation on Jell-O consumption. The city leading the nation in putting away the jiggly stuff is Salt Lake City, closely followed by Des Moines, Milwaukee, and Pittsburgh, with Tulsa and Oklahoma City tied in fifth place. Investigators at the Oklahoma State University Tulsa County extension offices stated they believe the high number of church pot-luck dinners in these cities accounts for the statistics.

Freeze Your Assets

- Most of us put out our Christmas trees for the mulching crews after the holidays, while others plant live trees in their yards. The people of Nome, Alaska, however, actually turn their trees into a forest. The "arboreally challenged" city has a surplus of frozen harbor acreage that time of year, and hearty citizens haul Christmas trees there and get out the ice borers. The result is an overnight forest of spruce and fir trees which is inhabited by plywood bears, walrus, and reindeer and serves as a course hazard for the annual March golf tournament during the Iditarod Trail Sled Dog Race. The biggest hazard is that out-of-town pilots who land on the ice try to secure their planes to the trees.

All-Time Greatest Product Bombs
And Who Can Wonder Why

- Country People/City People: The first anti-pollution shampoo, 'specially formulated for the pollution where you live. But city folk won't buy it in the country, etc.
- The smokeless cigarette. A huge success with non-smokers.

Who Says There Are Too Many Lawyers

- Shayna Beevers of Gretna, Louisiana, made adoption history last year when she formally adopted her Cabbage Patch Doll, Jeanette Abby, in domestic court. Testifying before the judge that the doll was well cared for with her own crib in the parental bedroom and use of Shayna's own high chair, she also stated that the doll would be supported by Wally Beevers' American Express Gold Card and her personal allowance. Wally Beevers, Shayna's natural father and the doll's adoptive grandfather, issued a statement that a formal adoption would be best for all parties concerned and agreed to continue subsidizing Jeanette Abbey's care until Shayna reaches the age of majority. Not surprisingly, Beevers is an attorney.

Climb Every Mountain

- Scientists have released their findings that mountains exist on the Sun. While it may seem a little odd that a giant ball of flaming gases might be the home of a toasty-warm St. Moritz, the mountains are in reality closer to "large bumps" about five times the diameter of Earth and a third of a mile high. The interaction of boiling gases and the star's huge magnetic field combine to form the masses which may be referred to as "mountains on the sun."

Go With the Flow

- About 100 tourists a day cram themselves into a temple in Kanchanaburi, Thailand, to view a modern miracle of meditation and synchronized swimming. For four years, a 52-year-old Buddhist nun by the name of Anong has descended into a pool in the temple 10 times a day, floating tranquilly on her back while assuming the cross-legged pose of Buddha in meditation. Observers exclaim that her face never falls below the surface of the water even though she doesn't tread water or touch the bottom of the 6-foot-deep pond. The nun attributes her buoyancy to concentration and pond spirits. Tourists pay 40 cents each to view the spectacle.

Quick Facts

- Rice is the primary staple-food of more than half the world's inhabitants.
- Leno and Letterman have a long way to go. It is estimated that Johnny Carson cracked more than 600,000 jokes while he was the host of *The Tonight Show*.

The Sweet Smell of Success

- City Council members in Independence, Missouri, recently protected the rights of citizens to be free of the presence of people "who are unruly, noisy, or disrupt meetings by 'creating a noxious or offensive odor'" by passing an ordinance against those things. While we may breath a collective sigh of relief that the rest of us finally have legal recourse against those who may have forgone a weekly bath or overindulged in garlic and chili, Independence officials were quick to point out the "noxious or offensive odors" they were talking about really meant Mace, pepper spray, or stink bombs.

What, No Shoulder Pads?

- A newly wealthy businessman in Romania named Alexandru Ilie saw his capitalist dream come true when he built a full-scale copy of the Southfork Ranch of TV show "Dallas" fame. Fond of wearing cowboy hats, Alexandru helped meet expenses by charging $1.60 for tours through the spread. While many Romanians no doubt are thrilled at a little bit of the Old West in eastern Europe, we hope they can overlook that famous wrangler landmark replica of the Eiffel tower in his front yard.

Throw Out That AbBuster

- Single men of the Dinka tribe in Sudan believe the way to a girl's heart is through fat. They gorge themselves on milk for more than three months every year before a contest in the fall to find the fattest man in the country. Rolls of fat and a double chin are believed to be a prime indication that the guy is a real catch—that shows that his family's cattle herd is large enough for them to spare all the milk it takes to feed him. During the last competition, the eligible mayor of the town laid on a papyrus mat for 12 weeks and consumed five gallons of milk a day.

Miscellany Mania

- Recently, a radio talk show host was angered by the fact that someone had attempted to register a pig as a presidential candidate. The host railed that a pig was incapable of doing the job. "They just sit around all day," he said. "Anyone knows they should have registered it for vice-president!"

- Catsup, or ketchup, came to us from China by way of Great Britain. The Chinese made a spicy fish sauce that was adopted by the Britons. The British added tomatoes to the mix, and our present day sauce was born. Catsup was sold as medicine back in the early 1830s.

4

SON OF TRUTH IS STRANGER THAN FICTION

By J.C. Walker

Sock It To Me

- Two men in Marquette, Michigan, recently participated in the World Winter Cities Forum competition for creative design in ice shanties. With the help of cooperative local laundromat owners, the two built an ice fishing shanty made entirely of unmatched socks. Dubbed "Socked In," the construction sat alongside other participants such as a 10-by-16-foot aluminum mermaid and a 12-foot-high snowy owl.

The Things We Do For Love

- A Boston College professor has proclaimed himself to be the country's expert on kissing, having written two books on the subject. He's reported to have discovered at least 25 different types of kisses, including his own technique of keeping his eyes open in the clinch. He also documents statistics that Americans on average kiss for less than a minute at a time, although the national championship goes to a kiss

What We Do For Love

that lasted 200 hours. Unfortunately, the professor admits that his interest turned academic when most of his own kiss recipients told him, "You've got to be kidding."

No Ifs, Ands, Or Butts

- Officials in Birmingham, Alabama, recently began distributing pocket ashtrays free to citizens in an effort to curb the smokers' habit of flinging cigarette butts onto the ground.

Mud-Slinging Politicians

- Officials in Hanford, California, are on the record for maintaining an old law that forbids adults from restraining children from jumping in mud puddles. Hanford police report they have never had to enforce the law, which would result in a police record for a perpetrator.

Be My Honey

- Brewers in Vermont are reviving a beverage that was discovered long before grape wine or beer—mead. Mead is wine made from honey, and increasing amounts of it are being produced in meaderies around Stowe to meet the rising demand. Brewers promote it as a healthful after-dinner drink and educate buyers as to its 8,000-year history in Europe. The largest mead producer is in California, which, after 30 years of mead production, puts out about 7,000 cases a year. The American Mead Association reports that it was the favored drink of King Arthur's court where it was generally regarded to be a powerful aphrodisiac. Federal regulations prohibit mead producers from making that claim today.

Hot Stuff

- Students at Pattonville High School in Maryland Heights, Missouri, can rightfully say their school days are full of hot air—their school is heated by methane gas from a nearby landfill. A 3,600-foot pipeline carries gas to the school where it is used to keep the building at a comfy 70 degrees throughout the school year, and students say they don't even think any more that the heat in their classrooms comes from rotting garbage. The methane gas was made available to the school district by the landfill company, which was already using the methane to heat an asphalt plant and a commercial greenhouse and to heat water for a concrete plant.

The Daily Grind

- Don't you just hate it when winter weather keeps you from your workout? The owners at the Knutson miniature horse ranch in Wakonda, South Dakota, did, too, although in their case they were concerned about exercise conditioning for their collection of 140 miniature horses. The solution was to purchase three used, exercise treadmills. Every day in winter, eight of the 30-inch-tall critters jump up on the machines for a 45-minute workout at 2 miles per hour. Times continually expand as their condition improves, and Lyle Knutson is looking for another used treadmill. Apparently the horses have developed preferences for which treadmill they like to use, limiting the number of horses that can be exercised every day.

Forget "Baywatch"

- A young female was rescued recently when she fell through the ice in a frozen pond outside Topeka, Kansas. Authorities were alerted by her sister and came to the rescue. The story started to attract attention only later when it was announced that the victim was Shammy, a 24-year-old mare who was pulled from the pond by firemen after her sister, Giyana, stomped and whinnied outside their owner's home until he came out and saw the first horse in the ice.

Flipped Out

- City officials in Olney, England, feted the winner of the town's annual pancake race last winter. Avril Soman beat the times of 12 other women with a race of 63.5 seconds, travelling 415 yards with a skillet in her hand. The race commemorates Pancake Day, also known as Shrove Tuesday, which is the last day for revelry before Lent. Participants must flip a pancake in the frying pan at the beginning and at the end of their sprint, with the record time being 58.5 seconds. According to the customary explanation for the observance, it started in 1445 when a woman, realizing she was late for services, rushed into the church holding a skillet with a pancake in it. The traditional prize for the winner of the race is a kiss from the vicar.

Truth, Justice, and...

- Captain America lives! Yes, it's true: John F. America of the United States Marine Corps was recently promoted from artillery officer to captain at Camp LeJeune, North Carolina. "I would be lying if I said people didn't notice it," he said. "But people will remember it whether I'm screwing up or doing something right."

Greens With Envy

- If you've had enough of the usual New Year's Day celebrations, think about a trip next year to observe the Ayden, North Carolina, Annual Collard Festival. Featuring a beauty queen competition and a cooking contest, the event commemorates the southern custom of dining on collards on New Year's Day. The cooking contest features a variety of tantalizing collard recipes and has produced unforgettable entries such as the five-layer collard cake —alternating layers of corn bread and greens, garnished with hunks of steamed okra. The Collard Queen wins a $350 scholarship and the right to hold the title for the following year.

Bull Run

- Talk about an unforgettable vacation, not to mention getting more than you paid for. A recent service trip to Mexico by Anderson University freshman Paul Von Tobel was not exactly what he'd planned on. He purchased a truly unique memento of his experience, a full-sized, wall-mounted, stuffed bull's head with electrified lights for eyes. He didn't think much about it when he joined fellow students on the plane to return home and strapped himself in for takeoff, nor did he realize he might have a problem when Mexican officials stopped the plane on the runway and told everyone to get off to claim their luggage. When he returned, he was alarmed to see his prize on the floor, and when he went to retrieve it, he was grabbed by police and hauled off the plane to a small "ambulance type car." After several hours of halting interrogation by officials (Von Tobel does not speak Spanish), he was told he could go with his treasure after showing them the item did not contain a bomb. Even though the head had passed through security checks several times, the officials then interrogated the bull by grabbing the horns and shaking the head, apparently, to extract the electrical system. "I was getting really nervous because it is really fragile, and they thought the horns would come off," Von Tobel said. Apparently, his protestations finally worked because after 45 minutes another official entered the room, grabbed the student and his souvenir, pulled them outside and pointed at the plane. Von Tobel had to run with the bull's head under his arm to catch the flight before the plane left the runway.

Chicken Scratch

• Just when you thought the news couldn't get any weirder—this just in. An animal hospital in Jackson, Michigan, recently released the news that doctors there had fitted a rooster who had lost his legs to frostbite with artificial legs. Dubbed Mr. Chicken, the patient is reported to be adjusting nicely to his prostheses and is looking forward to the companionship of 14 chicks to be provided as part of his rehabilitation.

End of the Line

• Have those trips to the mall become dreary and predictable? Looking for a gift for that hard-to-shop-for friend or relative? The Los Angeles County Coroner has the solution to all your gift-giving problems: its own gift shop called "Skeletons in the Closet." The shop is hidden away in a small office on the Department's second floor, but it was swamped with eager shoppers last holiday season. They snapped up T-shirts, hats, mugs, note pads, and beach towels, all stamped with the official L.A. County Coroner's seal. Similiar products bearing the image of a chalked body outline were also fast movers. Shoppers looking for unusual stocking stuffers found racks loaded with aprons printed with "extra hands" and "spare ribs," as well as the always-popular personalized toe-tag key chain. The shop has also expanded to a catalog division and has exclusive distribution rights to sell coroner items internationally. One frequent shopper, a local funeral director, said of the shop, "This lightens things up a bit. Death is not a bad thing, it's a part of life."

Save Yourself

- The Royal Air Force helicopter rescue team braved gale-force winds and the freezing temperatures of the Snowdonia mountain range of North Wales to bring in a man who was reported to be crouching on an inaccessible mountaintop. When they were finally able to land, however, they were greeted with questions as to why they had come. Apparently, the "victim" was instead a Buddhist on retreat who had decided to observe the winter solstice in splendid isolation, at least until he was spotted by some hikers who thought he had climbed his way into a corner. He apologized profusely for having put out the team on such a miserable night, but declined their invitation to return with them. They left some hot drinks and extra food, and the meditating mountaineer returned to Anglesey the next afternoon.

And More of the Daily Grind

- And if you're having trouble visualizing teeny little horses running on treadmills, then try to imagine full-sized roasting turkeys sprinting in place. Yep, scientists at Harvard are watching male turkeys work out on treadmills to determine the interaction of tendons and muscles after the birds are fitted with tiny strain gauges and electrical flow sensors. "I've clocked them at 15 mph, or slightly better than a four-minute mile," said one scientist.

Felonious Strangeness

- A man in Texarkana, Texas, recently thwarted a car-jacking when he observed his assailant's pants were worn low slung on his hips. The victim hit the man over the head with a flashlight, pulled his pants down to his ankles, and drove away as the perpetrator struggled to stand up.

- Police in Portsmouth, New Hampshire, are seeking psychological testing for a man recently charged with robbery and two counts of criminal restraint. He held three people hostage in the Sheraton Hotel by claiming the candy bar he had in his pocket was a gun.
- Three robbers in Starkville, Mississippi, were caught in the act when the heist didn't go quite as planned. Now, charged with attempted murder, the robbers began to have problems when one member of the gang fired the .22-caliber handgun and nothing happened. This gave the clerk time to grab his own pistol and start firing wildly, driving the robbers out in a spray of bullets. Their high-speed getaway was a bust, too —their car careened off the road and crashed just as the robbers were picking up speed to escape.
- The U.S. Border Patrol will tell you they've seen it all—and then, this happens. Patrolmen were flying their usual route above the Rio Grande River near Del Rio, Texas, when they saw an illegal alien who was apparently sitting and waiting for them to rescue him. They surmised immediately this was true because the person sitting on the levee and waving at them was wearing a clown suit, complete with white makeup, a blue nose, rainbow wig and baggy red pants. Just to make sure he was seen, the illegal also jumped up and down and generally clowned around—apparently, the border bozo had tired of his long journey from Honduras and decided this was the quickest way to be returned home.
- A drunk driver in Cromwell, Connecticut, was recently charged with sideswiping nine cars as he sped down local highways. His defense was that he had passed out and thought he was only dreaming about the accidents, not realizing it was actually happening to him.

5

CHRISTMAS AROUND THE WORLD
By Mona Lee McKown

Early Beginnings

- Christmas began as "Christes Masse," a religious festival originating with angels on the plains of Bethlehem singing "Glory to God in the highest, and on earth peace, good will toward men."

- In the year 350, Julius I, Bishop of Rome, gave the 25th of December as the specific date to observe the birthday of Christ. However, it was traditionally celebrated as early as the year 98, and Telesphorus, Bishop of Rome in 137, ordered that Christ's birth be observed as a solemn feast.

- With "Christes Masse" coinciding with other pagan festivals, it was difficult to keep the religious holiday separate from the pagan rites. From the middle of December to the end, the Romans observed Saturnalia, honoring their god of agriculture. There was much eating, drinking, and riotous celebration in the streets. The Persians feasted and set great fires in honor of Mithra, their deity of light. The pagan Teutonic tribes of northern Europe honored Woden by feasting and drinking during their Yuletide season, the time of the rebirth of the sun. Because of the intermingling of Christian beliefs and pagan rituals, George of Nazianzus denounced this mixing of celebrations. He declared that Christmas should be celebrated without excessive feasting, drinking and dancing. However, the church found it impossible to separate the pagan from the Christian, and so, it "Christianized" many pagan rituals. It is through this mixing that today's Christmas celebrations incorporate the use of candles, greenery and lights for decorating, the lighting of the yule log, the singing of carols, and gathering together for feasting.

A Midsummer Christmas

- Christmas in Argentina comes during midsummer when it is hot and dry. Christmas dinner usually takes place outside in the shade of a tree or on a veranda. The menu usually includes a roasted suckling pig and small pieces of steak rolled and stuffed with mincemeat, hard-boiled eggs, and spices. The day is spent quietly, with the main festivities being celebrated after New Year's. On January 6, which is known as Three Kings' Day, the children leave their shoes beside their beds, hoping to have them filled with toys by morning. They also set water and hay outside for the horses or camels of the Magi.

Christmas in Iran

- Iran is traditionally thought to be the home of the Magi. In Iran, Christmas is known as the Little Feast, with Easter being the Great Feast. During the first 25 days of December, a fast for the Christians of Persia is observed. No meat, eggs, milk or cheese are eaten. Christmas Eve is the last day of the fast. After a dawn mass on Christmas morning the fast is broken, and the festivities begin. Santa Claus is not recognized in Iran, nor is there an exchanging of gifts, but the children usually receive new clothes.

Santa Claus—The Reality

- In Myra, a city in Asia Minor, a remarkable young boy was made a Christian bishop. He was known as the Boy Bishop and was the real Saint Nicholas. Saint Nicholas loved children and was always very generous to them. Greece and Russia made him their patron saint.
- Saint Nicholas' name has had many transformations. In Latin it was Sanctus Nicolaus; in German, Sankt Nikolaus; and in Dutch, Sinter Klaus, the origin for Santa Claus.

Other Christmas Customs

- The use of holly as decoration has gone on for centuries. There are more than 150 varieties all around the world, and it has been used world wide in many winter festivals. Since it bears fruit in the winter, it has become a symbol of immortality. It has also become a symbol of the crown of thorns worn by Christ, the red berries representing His blood. In Denmark it is called Christ-thorn.
- In the United States there are three billion Christmas cards sent annually.

The Many Legends of Christmas

- Decorating our Christmas trees with tinsel comes from a beautiful legend. The legend says that many years ago a good woman with a very large family was decorating the Christmas tree. After every one had gone to bed, spiders came and added to the decorations. They crawled from branch to branch, leaving their beautiful webs on the Christmas tree. To reward the loving mother for her goodness, the Christ-child blessed the tree and changed the webs into shining silver.
- Trees have been brought into homes and decorated for centuries. Primitive tribes thought trees to be sacred and decorated them in their homes to bring nature indoors. The Egyptians brought the green date palms inside to show that life could triumph over death. The Romans decorated trees with toys and other small objects during Saturnalia. When these many cultures accepted Christianity, they still continued their customs, but eventually changed them to honor Christ. It was then that the evergreen tree came to show that Christ brings new life to the world after the long dark days of winter.

Christmas at Home

- On Saint Nicholas Day, December 6, 1492, Christopher Columbus entered the port of Bohio on the island of Haiti. He named the port Saint Nicholas. The *Santa Maria* had been wrecked on a sand bank, and the chief of the island sent his men and canoes to help the strangers. The natives prepared their guests a feast of shrimp and bread. According to records,

Columbus was the first European to receive gifts during the Christmas season in America.

- In December of 1606, Captain John Smith spent the first Yuletide in the new world as a captive of the Indian chief, Powhatan.
- The Dutch on Manhattan celebrated Christmas with joy. Gifts, decorated trees, feasting, and religious services were an important part of the Dutch and their Christmas spirit.
- In Bethlehem, Pennsylvania, the Moravian settlements were busy during the weeks before Christmas. The women prepared Kuemmelbrod, sugar cake, mince pies, and Christmas cookies by the dozens. The Putz, a miniature landscape of moss, greens, toy houses, trees and animals and the Holy Family, was put under the tree.

A British Christmas

- During the Victorian era, new ways of celebrating were added, such as exchanging Christmas cards and having Christmas trees in homes.
- The English have celebrated Christmas for more than 1000 years. In time long past it was a holiday celebrated with hearty feasting and merrymaking. At one time Christmas was celebrated for a full 12 days each year, with each day having its own name and special ceremony.
- The Puritans banned Christmas in the mid-1600s until the monarchy was restored in 1660. At that time the celebrations became more spiritual.
- King George V sent a Christmas message to all parts of the British Commonwealth. This tradition has continued in recent years when the Queen broadcasts her Christmas message all over the Commonwealth.

Italy at Christmas Time

- Christmas in Italy is a highly religious holiday. This holiday begins with a novena, a nine-day period of special church services, ending on Christmas Eve. Christmas Eve and Christmas Day are days strictly spent with families. December 26, St. Stephen's Day, used to be a day of religious devotion. Today, the day is spent visiting friends and relatives, sharing gifts and holiday foods. It is also a day on which many families travel around viewing the many wonderful nativity displays. The Christmas season continues until January 6, which is Epiphany.

- The exchanging of gifts occurs on many different days, depending on the area of Italy in which you live. Along the Adriatic coast, Saint Nicholas' feast day is December 6, and it is on this day that Saint Nick visits the children. On December 13, Santa Lucia brings presents to the children in Sicily. Some families follow the tradition of exchanging gifts on Epiphany.

Still More Christmas Customs

- In ancient Britain, the mistletoe was a sacred plant of the Druids. During winter solstice, the priests and their arch druid performed many ceremonies around this sacred plant. Today, mistletoe is used as a means of obtaining a kiss from a girl who happens to be standing under it. In the language of flowers, mistletoe means, "Give me a kiss".

- In Lithuania, the Christmas Eve dinner table is covered with a layer of straw in memory of the night of Christ's birth in Bethlehem. An unconsecrated wafer, symbolizing the harmony, good will and love of the season, is shared by everyone in the family.

- In Newfoundland it is customary for the people of the area to "fish for the church" during the week of Christmas. They bring their catch to be sold for the local parish.

Jolly Ol' Saint Nick

- The steps taken to transform the lean saint to the jolly, chubby character we know today are many. When the Dutch first came to settle New Amsterdam (New York), they placed the image of their patron saint on their sailing ships. He was shown with a broad-brimmed hat and a long Dutch pipe. His long churchly robe was replaced by short breeches. In the early 19th century, the English influence on Christmas observances merged with the traditional parades of the Dutch in New York. In 1809, Washington Irving's writings pictured

Saint Nicholas as a jolly fellow riding in a sleigh pulled by reindeer. On December 22, 1822, Dr. Clement C. Moore wrote the poem "A Visit from St. Nicholas" for his children, which personifies the Santa Claus that we know so well today. On February 22, 1835, Washington Irving organized a literary society which met on December 6, 1835, to honor the famous Boy Bishop. The members smoked long Dutch pipes and participated in other early Dutch customs. The last step of Saint Nicholas' transformation came from the lively presentation by cartoonist Thomas Nast in 1863 in *Harper's Illustrated Weekly*. It was in this cartoon that Santa Claus was given his red fur-trimmed coat.

Home for Christmas

1620 In Plymouth, Puritans Ban Christmas

• In Plymouth, in 1620, the Puritans showed their dislike for the "pagan" festival (Christmas) by continuing hard work for the day and passing a law forbidding the celebration of Christmas. The Pilgrims, however, were somewhat less somber. When coming over on the *Mayflower*, they included a barrel full of ivy, holly, and laurel to decorate their tables and to make wreaths for their homes. Slowly, the attitudes toward the celebration of Christmas changed in New England, and in 1856 the day was made a legal holiday in Massachusetts.

A British Christmas

• An English Christmas dinner is normally served in the early afternoon. It usually consists of turkey, roast potatoes, mince pie, and plum pudding, decorated with holly and presented "a flambe" with brandy. The dinner is finished with candies, nuts and fruits. Later in the afternoon, tea is served with a healthy helping of rich fruitcake topped with a thick almond-paste icing.

More Italy at Christmas Time

- In southern Italy, Christmas trees are sometimes decorated with foil-covered chocolates and fresh fruits. Then on January 6, the children are allowed to eat the decorations.

A Labrador Christmas

- The children of Labrador receive little lighted candles which stand in turnips that are especially saved from the harvest for this Christmas custom. In earlier years the candles were made of deer tallow and were eaten along with the turnip. Today, however, the candles are imported, so the children miss this part of the tradition.

Quotes

- "The ideal Christmas gift is money, but the trouble is you can't charge it." *– Bill Vaughan*
- "What I like about Christmas is that you can make people forget the past with the present." *– Don Marquis*
- "If someone said on Christmas Eve, 'Come see the oxen kneel...' I should go with him in the gloom, hoping it might be so." *– Thomas Hardy*

The Last Look

- The most popular Christmas flower is the poinsettia. The Aztecs in Mexico knew this flower, but during colonial times, people noticed that the poinsettia bloomed only in December. It became associated with the birth of Christ. Dr. Joel Robert Poinsett, who was an amateur botanist and the first American ambassador to Mexico, sent cuttings home to South Carolina. Later, Albert Ecke was the first to grow the poinsettia commercially in the United States near Los Angeles. California now supplies most of the country with this beautiful Christmas plant.

6

THE OLD WEST

By J.C. Walker

The First Fact

- When we think of the Old West in American folklore, there is no more prominent figure than that of the cowboy. While movies and TV have convinced us that they mostly rode around the range, drank whiskey and sparred in an occasional gunfight or two—in reality, it was a hard, gritty life that would never have been characterized as glamorous.

Get Along Little Doggie

- The real test of the cowboy life was the cattle drive. Herds averaged 2500 head, and a dozen cowboys was considered an appropriate number to take them to market. Each man would have six to eight horses to ride during the adventure, and these "extra" horses would be cared for and protected by the wrangler. The trail boss acted as supervisor, and it was his responsibility to find a good resting place with water each night for the group. "Pointers" would get the cattle moving and then set the pace for the day. "Drag men" followed the cattle to hurry up stragglers and keep the herd together. Needless to say, these positions would change from day to day because 2500 herd of cattle can stir up a lot of dust! Fifteen miles of progress was considered a good day, and the tradition of cowboy singers began when cowboys on the night watch would sing to the cattle to calm them.

Old West Thought for the Day

- "I always make it a rule to let the other fellow fire first. If a man wants to fight, I argue the question with him and try to show him how foolish it would be. If he can't be dissuaded, why then the fun begins, but I always let him have the first crack. Then when I fire, you see, I have the verdict of self-defense on my side. I know that he is pretty certain, in his hurry, to miss. I never do."

– Ben Thompson, 1843-1884, Austin City Marshall

Clean Out that Attic

- One of the people most responsible for preserving many of the artifacts of the Old West wasn't a historian or a collector from the Eastern establishment, but an unlikely person—a pharmacist named Jim Gatchell. This true pioneer opened a drug store in Buffalo, Wyoming, in 1900, and quickly established a good name for himself with the frontier settlers and Native Americans alike because of his generosity and healing skills. The Northern Cheyenne considered him to be a great medicine man, often bringing him gifts, and as his familiarity with many Plains Indian groups increased, the collection grew to include many rare and treasured items. Before he died in 1954, Gathcell had collected irreplaceable photographs of the early days, along with the unusual items, and he had learned to speak Lakota as well. His collection was deeded to John Johnson County as the Jim Gatchell Museum of the West in 1957.

Listen Up, Pilgrim

- America's most beloved cowboy never rode the range at all, although he could claim that, as a boy growing up in southern California, he rode a horse to school. Marion Michael Morrison also had a pet Airedale named "Duke," from whom he later took the name. After narrowly missing admission to Annapolis, Duke attended USC on a football scholarship where he had the good fortune to meet up with movie cowboy Tom Mix. This famous buckaroo got him a summer job as a prop man for a movie in exchange for football tickets, and Duke capitalized on the opportunity by befriending director John Ford. Bit parts in 70 low-budget films followed, and Duke Morrison was on his way in a movie career. These notable cinematic triumphs had titles that the rising star in later years probably wished hadn't happened, such unforgettable titles as *Hangman's House, Rough Romance, Girls Demand Excitement, Men Without Women*, and *Ride Him, Cowboy*. Duke's real break came in 1939 with a film called *Stagecoach*, which made him a major star. Although he played dozens of cowboys and war heroes in movies until his death of lung cancer in 1979, Duke was well aware of the irony of his Oscar Award for his role in *True Grit* as Rooster Cogburn, a grizzled old lawman who was a parody of all the characters portrayed during the course of his career as a movie star named John Wayne.

Move Over, Madonna

- Times may have changed since the days of the Old West, but even then, there were superstars. Lillie Langtry was undoubtedly the first. She was born Emilie Charlotte Le Breton in 1833, daughter of the Dean of the Isle of Jersey in Great Britain, and she married Edward Langtry at 20. Lillie was an enterprising sort and captivated everyone with her beauty and wit. It soon became clear she would have to use both to support both herself and her increasingly uncooperative husband. Lillie mixed and mingled with the beautiful people and intellectual types in both Europe and America, and her singing tour of the West is legendary. She was also the "Madonna" of the era as well, refusing to abide by the lady-like standards of the day, and she was quite open about her close relationship with King Edward VII of England, as well as her friendships (often in "men only" clubs) with Oscar Wilde, Theodore Roosevelt, and Prime Ministers Gladstone and Disraeli. She produced her own beauty aids such as Lillie Cream, Lillie Powder and Lillie Bustles, and she was also available to endorse numerous other products as well. Judge Roy Bean is said to have been the first superstar groupie—a movie has been made about this adoring fan of Mrs. Langtry's who went so far as to name a town after her. With her stardom at its pinnacle, Lillie was reviled by critics, but was still hugely popular with the public, which allowed her to get on her own railroad train after performances and ride in air-conditioned luxury to her vineyards in Northern California to recuperate.

By George

- One of the most influential people in the Old West had a name we all recognize, but his contributions have been largely overlooked. At 22, George Westinghouse galvanized the railroad industry when he invented improved train air brake systems, later adding the first automatic electric block signal as well. George also invented a natural gas piping system; developed alternating current technology; patented a citywide telephone switching system; opened the world's first radio station; and was the first to give his employees a half day off on Saturdays, pension funds, and paid vacations.

Dodging Bullets

- One of America's first real boom towns was Dodge City, Kansas, and it earned its reputation early on as a rough place to hang up your boots—if you lasted that long. Six years after the establishment of Fort Dodge, a three-room sod house nearby became a resting place for buffalo hunters and traders passing through, and within a year the town of Dodge City was established, in 1872. The new railroad brought tremendous growth within another year, and suddenly a town of tents, stores, a dance hall, a restaurant and saloons sprang up where none had been before. The buffalo hunters continued to ply their trade, however, so one of the town's landmarks was the huge stacks of buffalo hides which lined the main street. The traders of this commodity were the principal clientele of the business establishments built to serve them—but their lifestyle stayed the same. Some Dodge City residents still say that the term "stinker" was coined to label the old-time buffalo hunters and traders who brought so much change to the area.
- Even though the hunters eventually decimated the buffalo herds in the Dodge City area, their presence before then made

a huge contribution to the lives of the residents. An estimated 850,000 buffalo were exterminated between 1872 and 1874, with hunters leaving carcasses by the thousands after stripping the hides. During hard times shortly thereafter, local farmers made the most of the situation by collecting and selling the buffalo bones to manufacturers of China and fertilizer.

- While the buffalo were gone by 1875, Dodge City continued to boom, thanks to the introduction of Texas Longhorn cattle. Five million head were driven to Dodge City between 1875 and 1885.

- Lawlessness predominated in Dodge City for many years, until law and order rode into town carrying the names of Bat Masterson, Wyatt Earp, Bill Tilghman and Charlie Bassett. It's thought that the famous but fictional character of Matt Dillon was a conglomeration of all these men. The lawmen took control of the situation immediately, having an ordinance passed in which guns could not be worn or carried north of the "deadline," the railroad track that divided the town. The south side was where "anything went" and probably was the origin of our expression "going south."

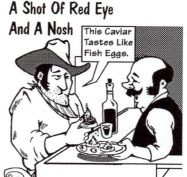

Get Your Ice Cold Beer Here!

- Dodge City may have been the wild west, but entrepreneurs knew potential when they saw it. In 1876 the town could boast a population of 1,200 and the presence of 19 establishments which provided alcohol. Ice was made in the town so that proprietors could offer mixed drinks, cold beer and even anchovies and caviar.

Gold Fever

- And what would the Old West have been without its Gold Rush? Actually, there was more than one, each with its own characters and legends. The Klondike Gold Rush of 1898 spawned some incredible stories of people who risked it all for fortune and fame.

- Clarence Berry was bartending in a Yukon saloon when a down-and-out Austrian miner asked him for a loan. He made the cash available and became the man's partner. Berry ended up with $1.5 million in gold from the claim, and later owned professional baseball teams in Los Angeles and San Francisco.

- Robert Henderson gave a hot tip to a brother-in-law that the tributaries of the Indian River were rich in gold. He was right, all right, but no one ever told him of the discovery on Bonanza Creek that made millionaires of others.

- W.D. Wood was the mayor of Seattle on a business trip in San Francisco when he heard of the strike and steamships full of gold at dock. He wired his resignation back to Seattle and left immediately for the Klondike.

- Frank Neill sailed around Cape Horn from Philadelphia to Juneau with 12 companions, but the trip was so difficult that everyone except him turned around and left . While he didn't strike gold, Frank made his fortune hauling logs to build the boom towns of the area, and he went back to Long Island to become even richer in the construction business. He did return to the Klondike, however, on his honeymoon.

- Martha Black was abandoned by her husband as they traveled to the Klondike, forcing her to hike, alone and pregnant, over Chilkoot Pass where she built a boat and sailed down the Yukon River. She gave birth in a log cabin. Later, she bought a sawmill, supervised 16 men on a mining claim and eventually became Canada's second woman to serve in Parliament.

- Jim Wallwork has the unfortunate honor of probably being the most unlucky pioneer in the Yukon. He and his crew hauled a small steamboat named Daisy Belle with teams of sled dogs over mountain passes from Edmonton to Dawton and the Yukon River. Once launched, the Daisy Belle was smashed to smithereens by the rough whitewater current of the river.

The Last Laugh

- Captain William Moore made his fortune in gold early on in the Rush, but had lost it all by the end of the 1880s. He built a cabin and claimed there would be a great gold rush in Skagway. He waited for the hordes to show up to build up a town around him. The only hordes who materialized were stampeders who claimed a right of way for a road on his property and drove him off his own land. Captain Billy had the last laugh, though—he was awarded a huge settlement that made him a rich man again in a court battle that went in his favor.

Trigger Happy

- The Old West still lives in the tradition of Fast Draw Competition. Actually, this particular activity didn't exist as a hobby until 1954 when a Knott's Berry Farm stuntman decided to time his fast draw using a single action six-shooter, a large clock-faced timer, wax bullets (fortunately) and balloons as targets. The World Fast Draw Association now claims the world's record fast draw goes to Gil Guerra, Jr. In the 1994 Traditional Elimination World championships in Deadwood, South Dakota, his record time of 0.255 included a reaction time of "approximately" 0.150 second.
- Sam Bass was born near Mitchell, Indiana, in 1851. About 1870, he moved to Texas where he was a cowboy, a mill hand and a deputy sheriff. He remained a deputy until 1875, after which he became an outlaw. He formed a gang, in the Black Hills town of Deadwood, South Dakota, whose purpose was to rob stagecoaches. In 1877, Bass and his gang robbed a Union Pacific train at Big Springs, Nebraska. They netted about $65,000. Sam Bass was called the "good badman" because he gave a portion of what he stole to the poor, much as in the legend of Robin Hood.

Criminal Quote

- "Old burglars never die, they just steal away." – *Glen Gilbreath*

7

FAMOUS COMEDIANS AND THEIR ACTS
By Mona Lee McKown

Can You Guess Who?

- William Claude Dukenfield was born on January 29, 1880, in Philadelphia. At age 15 William was already earning a living as a juggler. He later was very successful as a magician and a performer in vaudeville. In 1913, Dukenfield performed for King Edward VII at Buckingham Palace. In 1915, he made his first film, *Pool Sharks*. His career lasted for the next 28 years, in which he played as either a henpecked, bumbling husband or a small-time gambler and con man. William Claude Dukenfield died on a day which he supposedly hated—Christmas—in 1946. We know him as W. C. Fields.
- Benjamin Kubelsky was born in Chicago in 1894. At age 17 he began a very successful career in vaudeville as a violinist, but he soon discovered that he could drive an audience wild with his deadpan stare and graceful style. He starred in a few films, but it was his radio performances which caused his career to soar. He had his own radio program which was introduced in 1932 and was heard every week for the next 23 years. Then, in 1950 he transferred his show to television where it continued for another 24 years. Benjamin Kubelsky was better known as Jack Benny, and he continued to appear in theaters and nightclubs in the late 1950s and 1960s.

Thanks For The Memories

- Leslie Towne Hope left Eltham, England, with his parents when he was four years old. They took him to Cleveland,

Ohio, to live. Bob Hope, as we know him, made his first appearance on the Broadway stage in 1927. He continued his career as a stand-up comic, traveling the nightclub and small-theatre circuit between 1928 and 1932. In 1935, Bob performed on radio, and three years later had his own show. He appeared in some 60 films during his career

Vaudeville...The Start of It All

- The Marx family lived in New York City on East 93rd Street. They resided in a noisy apartment with an extended Jewish family of 11, along with a few other stray relatives. Their mother, Minnie, was the catalyst for their beginning a career in vaudeville. She promoted the family as "the Three Nightingales," "the Four Nightingales," and "the Six Mascots." Leonard, Adolph Arthur, Julius, Milton and Herbert were trained as musicians. They finally billed themselves as the Marx Brothers, Chico, Harpo, Groucho, Gummo and Zeppo. Minnie tried to control them all, but had little success when her sons got on stage. Once in front of an audience, their non-stop insanity, roughhousing and cutting up began. Their antics eventually evolved into a schoolroom theme with Groucho playing the part of Herr Teacher.

- During World War I, vaudeville began to decline, so the Marx Brothers went on tour with *I'll Say She Is*, a musical revue featuring Groucho as Napoleon. The show later opened on Broadway. In 1925, they performed *The Cocoanuts* by playwright George S. Kaufman and *Animal Crackers* in 1928. They performed the plays over and over again to raving audiences. The Marx brothers did so much improvising and ad-libbing that the plays were never the same two shows in a row.

- After the 1929 crash, the brothers moved to Hollywood and made 11 films over the next 12 years. Zeppo retired from the act in 1935. Three of the brothers continued, each using different characteristics in the act. Groucho always appeared with a cigar and a moustache and had a caustic wit. His nickname was attributed to his moodiness and the "grouch bag" where he kept all of his hoarded money. Groucho was the only one to develop a successful career away from his brothers. He became the host of "You Bet Your Life," which ran for 4 years on radio and 11 seasons on TV. Chico was the oldest, Minnie's favorite son. He played the piano and spoke with an Italian accent. Chico quit school at 12 years of age to work on the streets. He gained his nickname because of his success with the "chickies." Harpo played the harp, as his name suggests, and communicated only in pantomime.

- "The test of a real comedian is whether you laugh at him before he opens his mouth."   – *George Jean Natha*

Foreign Comedians

- Sir Charles Spencer Chaplin was born in London on April 16, 1889. He was a child star who appeared in music halls and did pantomime. He came to the United States in 1910 with a pantomime troupe and decided to remain. In 1914, he created his world-famous "little tramp," wearing baggy pants, enormous shoes, a bowler hat, and carrying a bamboo cane. He continued portraying this character in more than 70 films. As a tragic-comedian, Chaplin used a combination of techniques derived from the circus clown and the mime. Charlie Chaplin was not only a comedian, but also a director, producer and composer. He died on December 25, 1977, in Switzerland, where he had been living for several years.

Comedians of Today

- William Henry Cosby, Jr. did many one-man comedy shows in theaters and on college campuses. He was born in Philadelphia in 1937. He became known to television viewers in the weekly adventure series "I Spy," after which he did many television specials and two different programs bearing his name. His greatest success in television came with the creation of "The Cosby Show" in 1984. He created it and produced it. Bill Cosby has also hosted several animated shows for children, including "Fat Albert and the Cosby Kids" and "The New Fat Albert Show," in which he also provided some of the voices.

- Caryn Jones was born in New York City in 1950. She acted

in plays at the Helena Rubinstein Children's Theatre when she was 8 years old and continued there until she was ten. In 1974, she became a member of the San Diego Repertory Theatre and a member of the improvisational troupe, "Spontaneous Combustion." In 1983, Caryn went back to New York with her solo show, "The Spook Show," where she was discovered by producer Mike Nichols. Then, in 1984, her show was expanded and, with the help of Mike Nichols, it went to Broadway. The show was then called Whoopi Goldberg, after Caryn's professional name.

You've Said a Mouthful

- "There is not one female comic who was beautiful as a little girl."   – *Joan Rivers*
- "Life is a tragedy when seen in close-up, but a comedy in long-shot."   – *Sir Charles Chaplin*

Comedian Greats

- Jimmy Durante began his career as a saloon pianist, but opened his own nightclub in 1923. Durante was known for his prominent nose, which earned him the nickname "Schnozz." His quick wit and raspy singing voice helped him develop into a popular television personality.
- William "Bud" Abbott and Louis Francis Cristillo became the famous comedy team of Abbott and Costello in 1936. The comedy duo spent their first year together with a touring show, "Life Begins at Minsky's," a burlesque show. Abbot and Costello were always proud of the fact that their acts were never risque, as so many of the other burlesque routines were. Their first year together was the final year of burlesque. Then, with the help of their agent, Edward Sherman, they continued their careers in vaudeville. One of their most famous routines, "Who's on First," was performed on "The Kate Smith Show," a popular radio program in the '30s and '40s, giving the comedy team national exposure.
- Henny Youngman is one of the most unusual stand-up comedians of our time. His ability to deal out two-liners at five a minute with only brief pauses in between when he

draws his bow across his violin makes him one of the greats. In 1972, Henny taped 230 of his jokes to be used with candy bars dispensed from vending machines around Dallas.

Ain't That The Truth

- "This was some great act this guy had; Jack Benny carried a violin that he didn't play, a cigar he didn't smoke, and he was funniest when he said nothing." — *George Burns*

An Early Comedy Film Maker

- Mack Sennett became the father of film comedy as a director. Movie comedy started with Mack and the Keystone Films. The films were short, about 10 to 20 minutes in length. Many of the great comedians of the time worked for Keystone Film Company. Some of the comedy stars included: Mabel Normand, who was both beautiful and funny; Ford Sterling, with his heavy eyebrows and funny beard; Ben Turpin, with his overly crossed eyes; Chester Conklin, with his drooping mustaches, and Roscoe (Fatty) Arbuckle. Many wonderfully funny ideas were created at Keystone. There is much debate about who first thought up the idea of throwing a pie into the face of a comedian, but it was created at Keystone. "The Keystone Kops" were also a creation of Keystone and Mack Sennett. The basic story-line for the short movies was that whatever the Kops did (chases, collisions, accidents or races), they didn't do it right. They were always bumbling. Keystone prospered for a few years until movie goers began to demand more than fast-paced slapstick.

Quick Quotes

- "Funeral services were held this week for 82-year-old chewing gum magnate Philip K. Wrigley. In keeping with his last request, Wrigley's remains will be stuck on the bottom of a luncheonette counter." — *Jane Curtin*
- "If Shaw and Einstein couldn't beat death, what chance have I got? Practically none." — *Mel Brooks*

How—dee!

- Sarah Ophelia Colley was born in 1912 in Centerville, Tennessee. Ophelia grew up in a Southern home run by her genteel mother, who, Ophelia said, "was the epitome of a Southern lady." Her father was a gentleman of the South, not one of "drawing room upbringing," but one of the woods. He was a timberman who, along with his brother, had a lumber business in Centerville. Ophelia had four older sisters, the youngest one 7 years older than she. Ophelia's sisters called her "Ophie," and her father called her "Phel," which was pronounced feel. After graduating from Hickman County High School, Ophelia was enrolled at Ward-Belmont Finishing School in Nashville. She thought it was a good choice because of her interest in drama, and the school was supposed to have an exceptional drama department. Unfortunately, Ophelia felt totally out of place. She felt like a country hick at a European palace. Ophelia overcame her feelings of inadequacy and continued her schooling at Ward-Belmont. She studied drama and Shakespeare intensely. She graduated in 1932 and opened a studio in Centerville, teaching dramatics, piano and dancing. Then in 1934, she got a job with the Sewell Production Company. Her first production as a Sewell Girl was in *Dixie Blackbirds*, a typical minstrel style show. While on the road with Sewell Productions, Ophelia's salary averaged about $10 per week. Ophelia's career advanced to director for the production company. She traveled to various towns and directed plays in the local high schools. In 1937, after the death of her father, she quit work, angry and bitter at the world. Then in 1938, she began working on a character that would change her life, one who told country stories and anecdotes. Ophelia's character told the stories with a country dialect, and later began singing country music in an exaggerated, corny way. It paid off in April of 1939. She was asked to perform for the Pilots Club Convention in Aiken, South Carolina. Upon arriving in Aiken, she realized her new character should have some type of costume. Ophelia found a costume suitable for a young country girl who was going to a meetin' on Sunday. It consisted of a pale yellow dress made of organdy. It had a round collar and a grosgrain bow which was attached at the neckline with a safety pin. The top was sleeveless, and it had a self-belt. Ophelia also added white cotton stockings and a straw hat to which she added some big silk flowers. She wore white sandals, but later changed them to a pair of black "Mary Janes" with low heels and one strap. Ophelia's first performance was a huge success and carried her on to the Grand Old Opry where she became synonymous with her created character—Minnie Pearl.

The Last Fact

- In 1908, "Sober Sue" was introduced at New York's Victoria Theater by Oscar Hammerstein. Sober Sue's act consisted of standing on stage during intermission and Hammerstein's offering $1,000 to anyone who could make her laugh. Many people tried to get Sue to break into a smile, but everyone was unsuccessful. Sue's 10-minute act was such a huge success that soon the top comedians were trying out their best material on her. Hammerstein was able to benefit from the talents of these comedians free of charge. Little did they know that "Sober Sue" was not able to laugh because her facial muscles were paralyzed.

Sober Sue

8

PETS

By J.C. Walker

The First Fact

- Six out of 10 households in America include at least one pet, which can range from the usual cat or dog to the pot-bellied pig to the rare African iguana. The surprising fact, however, is that the rate for adoption of dogs has hardly risen in the past 10 years, while the popularity of cats has skyrocketed in that time. Cat ownership rose from 57,304,000 in 1987 to 65,765,000 in 1996, while dog ownership lingers around the 54,800,000 level.

The Cold-Nose Deduction

- People increasingly see their pets as members of the family, which is a good thing, because those four-legged children can often run up a substantial expense account. The American Pet Products Manufacturers Association estimates that the typical dog owner spends between $500 and $840 on Fido every year, excluding the costs of purchase and neutering.

How Much Does That Doggie In Your Window Cost?

KENNEL FEE $60
CHEW BONES $60
DOG FOOD $265
NEW RUG $125
VET $75.00

- Cats may not fetch, but they cost less to care for—about $390 a year, with $48 of that going to the purchase of kitty litter.
- Smaller furry friends are not necessarily cheaper to keep. A

pet chinchilla costs about $200 a year to maintain, after a purchase price of $380. Mice and rats are the bargain basement of petdom, costing about $5 each and $60 a year to keep.

- Owners of salt-water fish spend $180 a year on their pets, about twice the amount required for fresh-water-fish maintenance.
- Reptiles also run the gamut from upscale to bargain. The current rage for iguanas has increased the price to buy and keep them to about $220—usually twice that of their lizard cousins. Turtles are cost effective at about $107—and you'll have each other around for a while. Snakes are the designer product of reptiles—a new one will cost $160, and the lucky owner will spend $275 to keep it.

Chimp Change

- A longtime resident of Foster, Ohio, recently went into seclusion following his retirement from a lifelong career in sideshow entertainment. Sam the Chimp was housed next to the Train Stop Inn where he amused townspeople who watched him smoke cigarettes and drink beer. He also had a fondness for peanut butter sandwiches, apples and watermelon. Sam no longer makes public appearances. His cage was in the proposed location for the new City of Foster public restrooms.
- "A man was bitten by a dog. He was taken to the hospital. Some hours later, a man from the pound came to see him and give him the bad news that the dog was mad. The victim said, 'How do you like them apples? He bit me and HE'S mad?'"   – *Milton Berle*

Bullish on Fido

- Business is booming for an East Coast company that has moved far beyond the pet supply supermarket concept. Not content just to provide rawhide bones and grooming rooms to clientele, Best Friends Pet Resorts and Salons now boasts superstores with 15,000-square-foot environmentally controlled buildings which feature private patios, split-level kitty condos, full-service grooming salons, whirlpool tubs, indoor playrooms, and (for that aging baby boomer market segment), assisted care centers. It must be what two-legged and four-legged customers want because the company presented double-digit revenue increases last year.

Dog Paddling

- When disaster strikes, a big part of the job of the Federal Emergency Management Agency is to rescue animals as well as people. Very often citizens jeopardize rescue efforts by refusing to leave pets or livestock behind, perhaps, because animals frequently comprise a large portion of many citizens' livelihoods in devastated areas. In Washington during the massive flooding of late 1996, more than 400 animals were lost.
- "A small boy brought a dog home and said to his annoyed mother, 'Mommy, it only cost me a nickel, and for that we got a dog who's going to have puppies!'" *– Milton Berle*

Bet You Can't Eat Just One

- A man in Pomona, California, was recently cited for illegally transporting and showing a 350-pound African lion and a 300-pound Bengal tiger. The animals had been born and raised in captivity, but authorities were a little negative about the critters' full-time home—a converted Frito-Lay delivery truck.

Why Your Dog Thinks He's Human

- 94 percent of American pets receive regular medical supervision.
- 83 percent always eat premium pet food.
- 37 percent have regular teeth cleaning.
- 70 percent are on an exercise regime.
- 35 percent of pets are dieting at any given time.
- Half of all dogs in the U.S. go on errands with their owners.
- Half also have a bed of their own.
- 66 percent of dogs vacation with their owners, while 25 percent of cats do so.
- One third of American pets have special clothing or collars; the same number have a framed picture of themselves at home and are included in the family Christmas card.

- One quarter of American dogs have had a formal painted portrait done.
- 74 percent of all pets are cared for by the woman of the house.
- Most common names for all pets in order of popularity: Molly, Sam/Sammy, Bear, Brandy, Ann/Annie, Max, Abby, Buddy, Fluffy, and Jessie.

Rocking Around the Christmas Tree

- A startled family in Sapulpa, Oklahoma, found out the true meaning of a "living Christmas tree" last holiday season when their holiday decorations began to shake and tremble as they watched. After an afternoon's vigil, the group found the source of the tremors—a well-fed, well-disguised ground squirrel who was carried inside with the tree and then set up housekeeping there. Apparently, nursing a broken leg, the little guy had seized the opportunity to convalesce in yule splendor while recovering on the ample food and supplies left out during the holiday season. Local animal control authorities ended the squirrel's Christmas vacation by capturing him, setting his leg, and releasing him into the wild again.

Bats in the Belfry

- Pets aren't always necessarily cuddly. They may also have spiritual callings. Scientists in Ireland have discovered that distinct types of bats categorize themselves as Protestant or Catholic. Really. Natterer's bats like to nest in stone walls common in big Protestant churches, and the little guys prefer their warm-up flying space in the enclosed roof spaces of those buildings. Long-eared bats like to squeeze into cozy little nests between roof slates and beams, such as those usually used on Catholic cathedrals. Scientists have also found that lesser horseshoe bats have aristocratic leanings since they seem to like the big 17th-century homes that feature grand roof spaces in summer and cozy cellars in winter.
- "A man walked into a bar with a dog, claimed that the animal could talk, and offered to sell it. The bartender refused to believe the claim and was about to mark it all down to the

full moon when the dog said, 'Buy me. Somebody please buy me. My owner is mean and vicious. He's always kicking me and hitting me. I happen to be a great dog. I was in the service. I have three medals for bravery. Please buy me.' The bartender asked the owner, 'How could you sell such a wonderful dog?' The man answered, 'I'm sick and tired of his lies!'"
– Milton Berle

First Walkies, Now Talkies

- We've all heard about obedience classes for dogs (frequently heard to be an oxymoron), but would you believe there's a shopkeeper in Singapore who gives singing lessons for birds? People bring their caged birds every Sunday morning to a local cafe where the cages are placed in neat rows on pegs on the outside wall. It's a great social occasion with much conversation, coffee drinking and noodle consumption. The students are tiny lemon-lime colored wild birds called *mata putih*. By positioning newcomers with elementary singing skills next to a virtuoso *mata putih* tenor, the birds' individual musical skills improve. Periodically, an owner will jump up to re-position a cage in order to provide new or varied skills to a pet that needs improvement in certain singing techniques. Once the birds really get going and the pet owners have had a few rounds, neighbors complain the noise can become quite deafening.

He Followed Me Home: Can I Keep Him?

- The next time the kids beg for a pet, hand them the Viacom New Media YOUR INTERACTIVE PET DINOSAUR; TYRANNOSAURUS REX. Yes, there are now pet videos, not just videos for pets. This new game—er, pet—for kids features a 3D dinosaur that lives in the computer and needs his owner to care for him. By clicking at the right times with the computer mouse, kids can hatch, feed and play with their pet Rex. He also needs to be bathed and will respond to variable environmental stimuli selected cybernetically. The beast is programed to nag, too, as a dinosaur will demonstrate begging or pouting behavior if not properly cared for. Just to make sure Rex doesn't get bored, kids can give him a ride in the Jurassic Jeep or play a game of fetch. The dinosaur will help kids paint a cave wall and write dinosaur-friendly songs. And, of course, kids won't want their new buddies to be lonesome when off-line, so programs for five other dinosaurs are in the system, too. A special cyber photo album journal is thoughtfully included in order to preserve those precious memories and adventures with all the dino-friends.

Dogged Determination

- A hot book for the upwardly-mobile latte crowd is *The Seattle Dog Lover's Companion*. It's part of a new trend in books—travelogues for dogs. The author describes travels with—we are not making this up—his granddogs all over western Washington counties. Parks, beaches, and recreation areas are rated with a four-paw rating system, and real loser attractions rate only a picture of a fire hydrant. Thoughtful notations about off-leash areas and parks with tether and scoop regulations are cited. Of particular note are the features on the Top Ten Dog-Friendly Lodgings and the Top Ten Best-Smelling Parks.

Hold the Gravy

- Since pets are increasingly becoming part of the family in American society, they are also being included in holiday festivities as well. Veterinarians are raising concerns about the dangers of feeding dogs and cats meals from the Thanksgiving or Christmas table. Turkey and ham, for example, can be too rich for doggy digestive systems and can trigger pancreatic inflammation. Chocolate is ambrosia to humans, but it contains high levels of the stimulant theobromine which endanger canine heart and nervous systems. There are histories of an ounce of bakers' chocolate killing animals as large as 10 pounds. Turkey bones are always a problem, too. One surprising danger of people food to cats is the string which wraps the turkey during cooking—once it's tossed casually in the trash it becomes an inviting morsel to chew on, but presents real hazards to a cat's digestive tract.

Due Process for the 21st Century

- Law enforcement officials in Indonesia recently shocked the world as well as their own human-rights commission when they announced they would begin using venomous cobras to break up political demonstrations and compel suspects to confess to wrong-doing. Apparently, police have just had it up to here with violent crime in Bekasi, a Jakarta suburb, so they hired snake handlers to implement cobras as "poisionous weapons." One officer explained their actions by saying, "A human being is basically an animal with morality and ethics, and when he loses his morality and ethics, he will injure and even kill, like an animal."

9

THE UNUSUAL AND
THE AMAZING
by Kathy Wolfe

First Fact

- Some lightning bolts are up to 20 miles long, and their temperature can reach up to 30,000° Centigrade, which is five times hotter than the sun.

Think About This

- The rather unusual epitaph on the tombstone of a Mr. Alexander Woollcott read, "Here lies Alexander Woollcott who died at the age of 92. He never had imitation fruit in his dining room."

- A certain policeman spotted a car swerving erratically down the street one afternoon, and upon pulling the driver over, learned that the driver was blind. The driver's friend in the passenger seat was giving his sightless pal directions since he was too intoxicated to drive himself.

- During a Texas tornado, a man milking Bossy in the barn was given a little ride. The farmer, the cow, and the barn were lifted off the ground, and when they were set back down, not even a dribble of milk had spilled from the bucket.

- A fisherman fishing for the Marshall Islands' goby, the world's smallest fish, would have to catch nearly 18,000 of them to equal one ounce.

- Admiral William Leahy, a U.S. Navy officer, spoke to President Harry Truman in 1945 regarding the atomic bomb, "That is the biggest fool thing we have ever done.... The bomb will never go off, and I speak as an expert in explosives."

- "Never give advice. Look at Socrates, a noted Greek philosopher, who went around giving good advice ... and they poisoned him." — *Anonymous*
- Mother Teresa was once asked if she thought she would ever go to the moon, to which she replied, "If there are poor and unwanted people on the moon, I will surely take my sisters there."

Ponder These Facts

- If you're considered the "black sheep" of your family, you're supposedly worth less than the other members. This expression came into being because the wool of a black sheep cannot be dyed, and it fetches less money than regular wool.

- "If at first you don't succeed, try looking in the wastebasket for the instructions." — *Ann Landers*
- The average American sleeps away one-third of his life. But did you also know that he spends two-and-a-half years in the bathroom over the course of a lifetime?
- Adolph Hitler's favorite movie was *King Kong*.
- "In America, anyone can become president. That's one of the risks you take." — *Adlai Stevenson*
- The Animal Control Office of East Haddam, Connecticut, came up with what they thought was a clever new dog tag, one shaped like a fire hydrant. Their resourcefulness, however, was short-lived as they began receiving calls from owners of female dogs, claiming the tags were discriminatory.
- It seemed to be a problem-free escape plan to prisoners incarcerated in Mexico's Saltillo Prison. Just dig a tunnel that wound up outside the prison walls. After months of digging, the convicts finally reached freedom ... or so they

thought. They had angled their tunnel right up into a neighboring courtroom.

- "You can avoid having ulcers by adapting to the situation: If you fall in the mud puddle, check your pockets for fish."

  – Anonymous

- The state of Alaska has eight national parks.

- San Francisco resident Nicholas Scotti planned a trip to Italy to visit relatives. He boarded the plane, which made a scheduled stop in New York City. Nicholas was convinced he had landed in Rome, and spent two days tramping through the Big Apple in search of other Scotti's. During his search, he saw many signs written in English and heard many English-speaking Americans, but he thought he was seeing tourists. Since he was not fluent in English, his inquiries were difficult to understand. Needing directions to the bus depot, he met a policeman who happened to have been born in Naples, who answered him in perfect Italian, further reinforcing Nicholas' belief that he was in Italy. By the by, his error was found out, and he returned to San Francisco, but, alas, never having made it to Italy.

Interesting Info

- Los Angeles Lakers center Kareem Abdul-Jabbar scored 38,387 points in his basketball career. Kareem was originally known in the NBA as Lew Alcindor.

- In 1987, about 735,000 fax machines were in use. Eight years later, there were more than 17 million.

- A well-meaning Texas state legislator introduced a bill that would require a criminal to give 24 hours' advance notification to their victims as to the nature of the crime, and the time and place it would occur.

- One man starts driving west from New York City. Another man takes off from the southern tip of the border of Texas. Both drive at the same speed. The first man reaches Chicago before Driver #2 is even out of Texas.

- A rat can tread water for three days, swim up to half a mile, make 4-foot leaps, and squeeze through a half-inch hole.

- The Spanish word for "six"—*seis*—gives us our word *siesta*, which is a rest at noon, the old sixth hour of the day.
- Cartoon character Charlie Brown tells of his life's new philosophy, "I only dread one day at a time."
- Can you identify famous sisters Anastasia and Drizella? Fairy tale fans will recognize them as Cinderella's step-sisters.
- Your body uses 17 muscles to smile, while it takes 43 to frown.
- Budget Rent-A-Car was founded by Ann Landers' husband.
- "The scientific theory I like best is that the rings of Saturn are composed entirely of lost airline luggage." – *Mark Russell*
- Neil Armstrong was the first man to walk on the moon. Yet he was the only one from the Apollo XI crew not to write a book about it.
- An alarm sounded at a Brazilian police station early one Monday, alerting police that a local bank was being robbed. The station telephoned the bank to verify the situation; unfortunately, one of the burglars answered the phone, apologizing to the officer for the false alarm. He escaped with $3,700.
- Prior to the 1979-80 NBA season, there was no such thing as a 3-point basket. The first 3-pointer was shot by Chris Ford of the Boston Celtics.

More Interesting Info

- If you can score in the top 2% on an I.Q. test, you may be eligible for membership in Mensa, an international organization for people of superior intelligence, which requires an I.Q. "higher than that of 98% of the population."
- Every year, more than 100 million neckties are purchased in America. Knot these all together end to end, and you could go around the world three times.
- Rev. Charles Lutwidge Dodgson was a famous mathematics professor at Oxford. But it was not his lectures that brought him fame. It was a children's book he wrote under the name Lewis Carroll, *Alice in Wonderland*.

Data to Consider

- "The human brain starts working the moment you are born

and never stops until you stand up to speak in public."

– Sir G. Jessel

- World heavyweight champion Muhammad Ali earned upwards of $50 million in the boxing ring. His technique was to "float like a butterfly, sting like a bee."
- In 1950, when fear of Communism was at its height and shortly before the McCarthy hearings took place, a blacklist of those celebrities suspected of being sympathetic to Communism was published. They included Leonard Bernstein, Burl Ives, Pete Seeger, and newscaster Howard K. Smith.
- A gentleman in England noticed a cold draft while sitting in his living room and began investigating its source. When he had tracked it to a certain spot, he removed the floorboards, only to find a 1000-foot deep hole in the middle of the room. It appears the house had been built over a 200-year-old mineshaft, and although the man and his family had lived there for more than 20 years, the shaft had never been discovered.
- 291,557 men died in battle during World War II. 529,332 lost their lives in the Civil War.
- In 1977, the U.S. government allotted $2,500 to the city of Arlington, Virginia, to investigate why "people are rude, cheat, and lie on the local tennis courts." The city hired professors of sociology, ethics, and philosophy to determine the cause.
- Under pressure from the public, the city council of a small Michigan community lowered the legal age for driving a cab from 21 to 18. Only thing was, the town didn't even have any taxicabs.

Think About This

- Take an average person in his mid-30s and give him a credit card. Say this average person pays $25.00 in interest on that credit card every month. If that person invested that $25.00 every month, by the time he reached 65, he would have $57,200.

- Most people know that a bigamist is a person married to more than one person at a time. But do they know the alternative definition? ... a fog in Italy.
- A young man and his girlfriend had just had an argument, and he left her apartment in a huff. As he passed below her upstairs window, she dropped a 51-pound watermelon on him, breaking his right shoulder and two ribs. The watermelon made it without a scratch.
- In 1883, a baby girl was christened "Anna Bertha Cecilia Diana Emily Fanny Gertrude Hypatia Inez Jane Kate Louisa Maud Nora Ophelia Quince Rebecca Sarah Teresa Ulysses Venue Winifred Xenophon Yetty Zeus Pepper. This was a name for each letter of the alphabet, with the multi-monikered girl's surname beginning with "P" placed at the end.
- *The Wall Street Journal* defines a desk as "a waste basket with drawers."
- The cost of taking the 1990 census was about $10 per person for the entire population. This adds up to a whopping $2.51 billion.
- It was the finale of the opera *Carmen* being performed at the New York Metropolitan Opera House. The production included live horses pulling a carriage on stage. Unfortunately, the horses made rather a "mess" of things at center stage. As Carmen stabbed Escamillo in the final act, he stood back for her to die, which she did not. Confused, he stabbed her again, exclaiming, "Die! Fall, will you!" to which she replied, "I'll die if you can find me a clean place!"
- "My mind is made up, so don't confuse me with the facts."

– Anonymous

Interesting Info

- A German doctor claims that the human soul weighs 21 grams. He arrived at his conclusion by placing terminally ill people close to death on a very delicate scale and monitoring the scale at the precise moment of death, when, he asserts, the scale dropped 21 grams.

Ponder These Facts

- Have you ever been to Yerba Buena, California? If you've been to San Francisco, you have. Yerba Buena was its original name.
- Sources offer these tips to help avoid being mugged: Don't wear headphones with loud music blasting in your ears. (You'll never hear a mugger coming up behind you.) Stay alert at the cash machine. (Don't stand and count your money at the ATM. Take it to your locked vehicle.)
- Waiters refer to customers who sit at their tables too long as "campers." A senior citizen who spends an eternity getting through his meal is a "gummer."
- A person who puts a damper on others' fun is called a "wet-blanket." This expression stems from the fact that a wet blanket will put out a fire, much the same way a wet-blanket discourages a fiery spirit of fun.
- There are more homes in America with televisions than with indoor plumbing. Alan Corenk had this to say about TV: "Television is more interesting than people. If it were not, we would have people standing in the corners of our rooms."

10

WEDDING CUSTOMS AROUND THE WORLD
By Mona Lee McKown

How It All Began

- The custom of marriage dates back to the very earliest histories of man. In primitive times, man simply stole the woman he wanted for his wife, usually with the help of a strong-armed friend, who later became known as the "best man." The honeymoon came about when in ancient times the bridegroom had to keep his newly captured wife hidden, until her kinsmen grew tired of looking for her.
- Later in history, brides were bought by men, such as the "mail-order bride" or by a contract.
- Today, marriages are performed because of mutual love.
- The term "wedding" comes from the Anglo-Saxons. The word "wed" was the money, horses, or cattle which the groom gave to the bride's father as proof of his purchase.
- In ancient Israel, the bride was to wear a ribbon of blue on the border of her garment to show purity, love, and fidelity. From this, the custom of wearing "something blue" was developed.
- It is believed that the custom of having bridesmaids goes back to Roman times when there had to be 10 witnesses at a wedding ceremony.
- The custom of tying shoes on the back of newlyweds' cars goes back to the custom of giving away a pair of shoes to show that authority had been exchanged. The shoes showed

that the new husband now had authority over the bride and that her father did not.

- The tradition of carrying the bride over the threshold stems from the time when the bride was abducted from her family by her future husband.

- The bride stands on the left side of the groom during the wedding ceremony because of a tradition dating back to AD. 200 in Northern Europe. After capturing his bride, the groom was so fearful of the retaliation of the bride's family that he had her stand on his left, so his right hand would be free to use his sword, should there be a sudden attack.

Rice is For More Than Eating

- The custom of throwing rice at the bride and groom is found all over the world. In certain primitive tribes, people were actually married when they ate rice together. It was also used as a means of keeping evil spirits away from the newly married couple. Rice was also used as a symbol of fruitfulness.

With This Ring

- The Egyptians were the first to actually use wedding rings in marriage ceremonies. They were first used in the Third Dynasty of the Old Kingdom, around 2800 BC. The Egyptians believed that a circle represented eternity and, therefore, the wedding ring was a symbol of a marriage that would last forever.

The Egyptians Were First To Use Rings In Wedding Ceremonies

- Christians used the wedding ring in the marriage ceremony around the year 900.

- The ancient Greeks believed that a certain vein passed from the fourth finger of the left hand directly to the heart, so the wedding ring was placed on that finger.

- A wedding document, dated 1503 from Venice, lists "one marrying ring having diamond." The wedding ring belonged to Mary of Modina and is one of the earliest known betrothal rings which had a diamond. By the 15th century, the diamond ring became the most popular form of engagement ring in Europe.

- Pope Nicholas I decreed in 860 that an engagement ring was a required statement of nuptial intent for all Roman Catholics. For Pope Nicholas the ring had to be of a valued metal, preferably gold, for which the future husband would require some financial sacrifice.

A Fairy Tale Shower

- In Holland the first bridal shower was given many years ago. A young girl fell in love with a poor but well-respected miller. Since the miller did not have much money, the father of the future bride objected to the marriage and said that he would not give his daughter her dowry if she married the miller. The lovely girl and the miller were very upset by this decision. When the people of the small community heard what had happened, they decided that they would try to help solve this dilemma. None of the people had much money either, but they decided that if they each brought one gift, maybe the miller and his future bride would be able to marry. They gathered together at the young girl's house and "showered" her with gifts, such as kitchen utensils, linens and lamps, and she was able to marry the miller after all.

You Paid What?

- In January, 1964, a Masai chieftain offered to buy Carroll Baker, a blonde actress, for 150 cows, 200 goats and $750 cash. Usually, a Masai warrior spends about $200 and 12 cows for his new bride.

It Means What?

- The native women of northern Siberia would express their love for a man and indicate that they were available for marriage by throwing freshly killed lice at the prospective husband.

To Have Your Cake and Eat It Too

- The custom of the wedding cake began a very long time ago in Rome, about 1st century BC. Wheat had long been a symbol of fertility and prosperity and was used to shower new brides. Roman bakers, who were known for their confectionery skills, changed the practice of wheat throwing by baking the wedding wheat into small sweet cakes which were to be eaten, not thrown. However, the wedding guests were not willing to give up the fun of pelting the bride with wheat, and often threw the tiny cakes instead. Later in history, a compromise in the ritual developed in which the wheat cakes were crumbled over the bride's head. Then again later, a further change required the couple to eat a portion of the crumbs. During the lean times of the Middle Ages,the use of the tiny wheat cakes was changed again. The poor peasants were not able to use the once-decorative cakes, so they used simple biscuits or scones for the bridal party to eat. The guests were encouraged to bake their own biscuits and bring them to the ceremony. Any leftovers were then distributed to the poor.

Music to March By

- The wedding of Victoria, Princess of Great Britain and Empress of Germany, to Prince Frederick William of Prussia in 1858 started the wedding march tradition. Victoria was the oldest daughter of Britain's Queen Victoria. The young Victoria was a patron of the arts, and she valued the works of Mendelssohn and Wagner. When planning for her upcoming marriage, she chose the "Bridal Chorus" by Richard Wagner to be used as she marched down the aisle for the ceremony and the "Wedding March" by Felix Mendelssohn to be used as she and her new husband exited. After the wedding, brides all over Britain were using the wedding marches used by their monarchy.

Words of Marriage and Weddings

- "It takes two to make marriage a success and only one a failure."   *– Herbert Samuel*
- "In a happy marriage it is the wife who provides the climate, the husband the landscape."   *– Gerald Brenan*

- "Keep your eyes wide open before marriage, half shut afterwards." *– Benjamin Franklin*
- "There is no more lovely, friendly, and charming relationship, communion, or company than a good marriage." *– Martin Luther*
- "Men are April when they woo, December when they wed. Maids are May when they are maids, but the sky changes when they are wives." *– William Shakespeare*
- "Weddings seem to be magnets for mishap and for whatever craziness lurks in family closets. In more ways than one, weddings bring out the ding-dong in everybody involved." *– Robert Fulghum*
- "Let there be no more weddings. Get thee to a nunnery." *– William Shakespeare*

Unusual Wedding Traditions

- In the Marquesas Islands, wedding ceremonies are very unusual. It is a tradition in the Islands for the bridegroom to walk to his future father-in-law's house on a street paved with wedding guests. The guests must lie down on the street so that the groom can walk on their backs all the way to his future bride's home. If the wedding is small and not very many people are invited, then the guests must race from the back up to the front of the line to lie down again. After reaching the house the groom eats a raw fish that has been cut up on a human body. Gifts are then passed out, and there is a great feast. After the festivities, the human street is formed again, and the groom and his bride return to his home.
- In Bulgaria, Bulgarian woman were only allowed to have one bath in their lifetime. That one time was the day before her wedding.

Wedding and Funeral Combined

- In Madison, Wisconsin, Reverend Joseph Mueller was performing a wedding ceremony when he fell dead of a heart attack. Mueller's assistant, Reverend James Kaczmarek, immediately took over and completed the Wedding Mass and then administered the last rites to Mueller.

What is the Gift?

- The French Ministry of Education wanted to encourage reading, so they implemented a program that lasted from April 29 to December 31, 1972. The program consisted of presenting five free books to every couple who were married during those eight months. The newlyweds could choose between two different sets of French classics.

- Victor Emmanuel II was the first king to rule over a united Italy. However, this distinction is not what has made him famous. During his years of ruling, he collected a stunning collection of *ongles de roi* which he later presented to Countess Mirafiori when she became his bride. What is so special about his collection you may wonder? The collection was made from clippings of his big toe nail which he would let grow for a full year. The length of the nail would be at least one half inch. After the nail was clipped on New Year's Day, it would be given to the king's jeweler. The jeweler would then polish, shape and edge it in gold and encrust it in diamonds. In this way he was able to present his wife with a part of himself.

Celebrated Marriage

- Aurore Dupin was forced into caring for her strict grandmother, Madame Dupin-Francueil, after her own Bohemian mother had abandoned her. Aurore had been raised in convent schools and had led a very sheltered life on her family's estate in Nohant. After Aurore's grandmother died, her mother returned unexpectedly, claiming all her daughter's possessions.

- Aurore's mother tried to force her into marriage, and Aurore went on a hunger strike. She became sick enough that her mother finally gave up on the notion of an arranged marriage. Aurore was sent away for a few days to visit one of her father's old army buddies. While visiting James Roettiers du Plessis, Aurore met Casimir Dudevant. Aurore soon was captivated by the homely but elegant Casimir. The couple did not really court, but considered each other comrades. After on-again-off-again wedding plans, the marriage of the couple took place on September 10, 1822. Casimir was 27 and Aurore 18 years of age.

- The marriage was doomed from the beginning. Aurore was increasingly dissatisfied with her life and with the masculine role her husband had to play because of the dictates of society at that time. She discovered many interests not shared by her husband and felt that her life could be much more fulfilling.
- Aurore gave birth to a son and daughter and struggled constantly with her conscience. Finally, in 1931 she left Casimir and moved to Paris. It was then that she discovered her real genius, and under the pseudonym of George Sand, she stepped into literary history.

Not Even Near-Beer

- While we're on the subject of unusual weddings, a wedding in the Ukraine was so different that it made the international news. Apparently, the women of the village Lviv had had enough of their husbands' affinity for frequent nips of vodka, and alcohol was banned at public celebrations and on holidays. New Year's Eve was alcohol-free for the first time. According to the new village edicts, husbands who arrive at work obviously inebriated spend their days raking dung in a local pigsty. This has not been a hit with Lviv menfolk who are quite irate about their spouses' new-found determination. Resistence evaporated after one overindulged citizen who passed out in public woke to find his head had been shaved. The village womens' final *coup de grace* was a wedding which was, for the first time in the town's history, celebrated without drunkenness.

And the Color Is Perfect

- A young Norwegian couple got a wedding gift that will keep on giving. While traveling during their engagement in Belarus (part of the former Soviet Union), they learned of a congregation in the town of Berezino that was so poor it could not afford a church. David Holme and Ingunn Lyngset decided the best wedding present they could have would be to give the people who had shown them much kindness a church. When they sent invitations to their wedding last year, they included requests for cash donations rather than gifts. Although a few guests resisted, all eventually agreed and presented the bride and groom with $17,200 in cash, which has since been used to buy a building in Berezino and renovate it. Earlier this year, they returned with the second half of their wedding present, a load of construction materials to complete the overhaul of the building. The couple has no regrets about their decision: "We had to follow our hearts."

And Baby Makes Three

- Still, one of the most newsworthy weddings was that of Susu and Mike in Lopburi, Thailand. Dressed in golden clothes and jasmine flower garlands, they were married on TV, and recently announced the birth of a child. The happy couple are orangutans.

Beauty and the Beast

- After Edison's first wife, Mary Stilwell, died in August of 1884, he began looking for a new wife. Edison was by this time a millionaire and had become well-known nationally. Therefore, it was not a surprise that he wanted a wife who was just the opposite of Mary. He wanted someone who was sophisticated, bright and a member of chic society. Unfortunately, Edison was half-deaf, bug-eyed, plagued with halitosis and dandruff. Therefore, he caused many young women to turn away in dismay until he met a young girl from Ohio. Mina Miller was the daughter of Lewis Miller, a wealthy farm-implement manufacturer.

- The courtship continued a few months. Edison taught Mina how to use Morse code over the telegraph. It was by this means of communication that Edison asked Mina to marry him. She sent her reply the same way—yes.

Divorced Millionaire

- According to the *Guinness Book of World Records*, Thomas F. "Tommy" Manville, set the record for millionaire divorces— 13 of them. His marriage to his seventh wife lasted only 7-1/2 hours. He married for the last time when he was 65 years of age.

11

BABIES
By J.C. Walker

Here's Looking At You, Kid

- One of the most enduring American myths is that Humphrey Bogart, of all people, was the model for the famous Gerber Baby portrait that has been the company's trademark since 1931. If you have trouble imagining the well-known movie tough guy as that adorable face, you're right—Bogey was over 30 years old when that picture appeared for the first time on Gerber Baby Food jars. The myth is not without some basis. In fact, Maud Humphrey Bogart was a professional illustrator whose work was used by firms such as Prudential Insurance, Ivory Soap and *Harper's Magazine*, and she specialized in renderings of idealized cherubs with blond ringlet hair, button noses and frilly clothes. She also did some drawings of her young son that were used in a national advertising campaign for Mellin's Baby Food, so there is indeed truth to the claim that Bogey was a celebrity, even as a tiny baby.

Triple Threat

- Big Ridge Elementary School in Hixon, Tennessee, knows all too well that science marches onward. School administrators report that enrollment when school started in 1997 included three sets of triplets and six sets of twins in a population of 600. The National Center for Health Statistics recently released results of a study about multiple births which stated there were 4,594 sets of triplets born in the U.S. in 1994, more than four times the number born in 1971.

Fertility drugs are credited with the remarkable change, although all the mothers in Hixon reported their triple births occurred naturally. A teacher at Big Ridge says that she has her own ways of telling the three identical pupils in her class apart: "I just line them up and ask them to smile. Rebecca has no front teeth, and Blake is the tallest, so by process of elimination, that leaves Kathleen. If they separate and come to me one at a time, I haven't a clue."

Boom And Bust

- The Baby Boomers and the Baby Busters—where are they today? In 1995, Boomers made up 31 percent of the American population, while their children, the Busters, were 17 percent.

By Any Other Name

- The most popular girl's name in 1997 in the United States was Emily, followed closely by Sarah, Ashley, Kaitlyn, and Jessica. For boys, the winner was Michael, with Nicholas, Matthew, Jacob, and Tyler close behind. Some of the other names presently on the hit parade of top 50 choices by parents include: Courtney, Haley, Madison, Sierra, Bailey, Cassidy, Cheyenne, Deja, and Savannah for girls; and Cody, Connor, Logan, Devin, Tristan, Garrett, Dakota, Travis, Elijah, Caleb, Chase, and Hunter for boys.

Bear Hugs

- In a country with a billion people, two single births still managed to make the news. Baby pandas were born in 1997 in Chengdu, China, and although scientists were thrilled at the infants' progress, they were still apprehensive. "Bringing up pandas in captivity is very difficult," said Li Shaochang, director of the Chungdu Research Base of Giant Panda Breeding. Great effort is being expended by the Chinese government to preserve this shy and mysterious creature which has a justified reputation for being very particular about procreative matters. The number of pandas in the enormous country is now at about 1,000, and scientists believe without help they will be extinct in 40 years. If progress in captive breeding continues, "We can probably extend the existence of pandas on earth to 100 years or more," said Shaochang.

Mini Monkey Suit

- Planning that special event and worried that baby may not be properly outfitted? Don't be— there are companies out there which are more than happy to outfit your 14-month-old with his very own tuxedo. "We've even had one couple buy one so their child could go to the formal dining room on a cruise ship," they report, and specified features include a coat with tails, satin lapels, and, of course, a black

Mini Monkey Suit

satin cummerbund and a black ribbon-style tie. While you can't get one for your newborn or one in white, sizes do run from nine months to 4T and start at $57.95.

Sometimes Bigger Is Better

- The world of electronics has proudly announced its newest arrival—the baby computer. Sized to the scale of a stack of five credit cards, the teeny pocket organizer will remind you of your appointments, keep addresses and phone numbers, and obviously fit into a pocket. Reviewers, however, were skeptical about the little guy's potential for success: It's so tiny that there's room on its surface for only five buttons, so all information has to be input while the device is plugged in to a desktop personal computer.

You Are Getting Sleepy?

- Awake all night with a cranky baby? Then switch on the computer and tune in to The Fussy Baby Help Page. A desperate new father, Mike Lampkin, decided that he could use his graphics expertise to help other sleepless parents when he discovered that even week-old babies could see eight to 15 inches away and focus on high contrast shapes. What followed was "The Slideshow," a series of 12 black and white pictures with geometric art, happy faces, and lines which apparently give a squawking infant some baby food for thought. According to Lampkin, having the baby look at the doodles really does seem to do the trick. He also suggests printing out the pictures to post next to the changing table for less traumatic diaper interludes.

Be Kind To Your Web-Footed Friends

- It isn't a "man bites dog" story, but a headline in *The New York Times* "Breaking News" section did get attention: "Duck Hatches Chicken Eggs" took its rightful place next to the Mid-East peace talks and current airline disasters. Apparently, Clarion the Duck of Luthersburg, Pennsylvania, was the barnyard outcast in her social circle, and as a result, the clutch of eggs she was trying to incubate was infertile. Clarion responded to her overdue gestation by falling into a deep depression and, according to her owner, "was moody and wouldn't eat." Thinking it would help her emotional state, he slipped some fertile chicken eggs in her nest, and Clarion was a new duck once the babies hatched. Her joy was short-lived, however, as her offspring refused to participate in swimming lessons.

Bearing Gifts

- Bored with sending flowers, candy or telegrams to the baby who has everything? Then, consider wiring a message that's in step with the newest gift-giving trend—send a Bear Gram. Properly outfitted and accessorized, each teddy bear brings an appropriate greeting for the event or holiday and may include flowers and small packages.

Pomp And Circumstance

- Your baby can be officially greeted by none other than Bill and Hillary Clinton. Just send them a note with the baby's name, address and birthdate, and he or she will receive a letter on White House stationery. Complete with the First Signatures and embellished with the Presidential Seal, it says, "Welcome! Your arrival is a cause for great celebration for those who love you. The future holds bright promise and opportunity for you. We wish you a joyful and healthy life!"

How Tallulah Bankhead Got Her Start?

• A little piece of Victorian memorabilia that has been forgotten by many is the Piano Baby. Piano Babies were porcelain bisque figurines in a variety of forms and shapes, depicting babies and toddlers in all their adorableness in an array of cute poses. American and European parlors usually had at least a few, and most, as you might think, were perched atop the family piano. A majority were made in Germany from about 1800 to the 1930s, and there was a Piano Babies revival in the early 1970s with many of the old forms reproduced and baby originals fetching hundreds of dollars.

One Hump Or Two?

• A recent arrival at the Cleveland Zoo was cause for celebration—Laura and Palmer beamed over their new, 75-pound offspring named Cody. The seven-year-olds weren't newsworthy because of their early parenthood, but because of their species: all three are Bactrian camels. While it may not seem like a big deal that these camels with one hump (rather than the two of Arabian camels that we usually think of) are procreating, biologists are pleased. Cody will have a much easier time of it than his few remaining relatives in the wild—it's estimated only 300 to 500 still live in central Asia and Mongolia.

This Little Light of Mine

• Scientists have known for many years that adult fireflies glow in the dark to attract mates—but why would baby fireflies (larvae to you and me) do the same if they were not ready to breed? Entomologists at the University of Delaware released research indicating that rodents learn to associate a bitter taste with glow-in-the-dark dinner entrees, and subsequently avoid them. Luminescence is the larvae's way of advertising it's not an appetizing meal to predators.

Calvin Klein, No Doubt

• Even premature babies aren't overlooked in today's

marketing madness—a firm catering to young parents offers a catalog that includes "The Isolette Layette—a complete set of clothing for the well-dressed preemie!" Sizes start at TINY for infants who weigh one to two and a half pounds, and go up to MEDIUM for babies three to four and a half pounds.

Weighty Issues

- Eight pounds, nine pounds, 10 pounds…if it seems from recent conversation around the water cooler that babies are getting bigger, it's no coincidence. They are. Babies who weigh over eight pounds, 13 ounces are considered to be "outside the norm," and the incidence of babies that size or bigger has skyrocketed in the last two decades. *The Journal of Reproductive Medicine* recently reported that babies in that category were three percent of all live births in 1970, yet by 1985 their numbers increased to 14 percent. Experts believe that improved prenatal care and nutrition are probably the main reason, in addition to the significant drop in smoking. Women who are diabetic or obese are more likely to have big babies, and prenatal care has been a major factor in helping them have successful pregnancies and births, too.

- Dieting experts also have some sour news for heavy parents and their kids—a parent's weight is a more significant indicator of his or her child's inclination toward obesity later in life than that child's weight at birth. A study in the *New England Journal of Medicine* reported that a tendency to carry extra weight is inherited not only through genes but by shared eating and exercise habits. At age one or two, an overweight baby has an 8-percent chance of growing up fat if both parents are average or normal weight—but if one parent is obese, the chance is 40 percent.

Shoot First, Ask Questions Later

- The State of California is sponsoring a huge program of Baby Track and Field Events. Early scouting for future Olympic stars? Not even close. The "competitive events" are really a way to publicize the soaring increase in the incidences of pertussis and other childhood diseases, the direct result of parents neglecting to have their children immunized. In between the "Diaper Derby" events are animated lectures on the importance of giving babies and toddlers their shots at appropriate intervals. Organizers are hugely concerned that young parents often don't understand the importance of the immunization program; they estimate that over a million California children are still unprotected.

Word Of Mouth

- Parents have long wondered how children suddenly seem to "spout" words when they begin to talk intelligibly. Researchers at Johns Hopkins University have discovered that at about eight months children start to recognize words they hear frequently, and file them away for later use when they have the cognitive and physical ability to begin talking. These findings also emphasize the importance of conversing with even very young children. The scientists used two lists to test a group of babies for word memory—one contained 36 words used in stories read to them, and the other was a list of words not in the stories. The test babies sat between two speakers which were topped with lights. The lights attracted their attention, and then, words were read through the speakers. "We found they listened significantly longer to lists of words from the stories," researchers reported, "and the two-week delay between the stories and the words proved that the babies were remembering the sounds."

A Totally Unrelated Fact

- Kansai Obuchi, of Japan, died peacefully at the age of 72. But that's when the real excitement began. Obuchi was an avid chess fanatic during his lifetime, and in his will he left a strange request to his surviving loved ones. He specified that certain family members should meet at his home and pair off in chess games using any of the many fine sets he had collected in his life. Obuchi then specified that when the family tournament was over, the winner would be rewarded with the dead man's estate.

12

FACTS, DATA AND TRUTH
by Kathy Wolfe

Fascinating Facts

- King C. Gillette was preparing to shave one morning and found his razor in need of sharpening. It was then that the idea of a disposable razor blade hit him. After obtaining a patent in 1901, he had to wait until 1903 to make any sales, when 168 blades were sold. One year later, his sales were 90,000.

- The longest NBA game in history was decided after six overtimes. It was in 1951, and the Indianapolis Olympians finally defeated the Rochester Royals 75-73.

- Babe Ruth was once rushed to the hospital immediately following a baseball game, during which he had consumed 12 hot dogs and 8 bottles of soda pop. It was back to normal for the Babe after a good stomach pump.

- Jeans have been around since the 1850s when a 21-year-old Bavarian immigrant, Levi Strauss, fashioned the first pair out of the same brown canvas that was being used for wagon covers. They were originally dubbed "waist overalls" and could be had for 22 cents. San Francisco Gold Rush miners were his first customers since they needed the toughest pants that could be bought. Strauss' product name was born as the prospectors began asking for "those pants of Levi's."

- While mingling among the other guests at a party, a certain physician was becoming rather annoyed when several people began outlining their various symptoms and illnesses to him, asking his advice. As he complained about it to a gentleman he had just met, the other man urged him merely to hand over a business card and politely inform the freeloaders that "free advice is worth every cent it costs." Later in the week, as the doctor went through his mail, he happened upon a bill for $500 for "professional services." As it turned out, the doctor's new acquaintance at the party was a lawyer.

True-Blue Truths

- Taking a shower will use up only half as much water as taking a bath.
- The Ford Motor Company was started with only $28,000 and 12 workers.
- We often think of a truffle as a creamy chocolate confection, but it is also the name of an expensive delicacy, a fungus that grows underground. Its outside is black and warty, and it usually grows near oak trees. It is hunted by pigs called "rooting hogs" who sniff out the truffle.
- Who would think washing dishes could be hazardous to your health? An unfortunate fellow from West Germany was busy at this task when he blacked out briefly, toppled forward into the sink, and drowned in his own dishwater.
- During its first five years of production, more than 32 million plastic eggs filled with Silly Putty were sold.
- At England's Health Exhibition in 1884, Thomas Crapper introduced his latest invention, paving the road to indoor plumbing ... the flushable toilet.
- Because he had determined that a certain movie was too long, a creative theater manager made the decision to edit it himself, eliminating all the movie's songs. Unfortunately, the movie was *The Sound of Music*.
- A newspaper poll in Alabama asked the opinion of its readers on this subject: "If you had one extra place in your fallout shelter, who would you give it to?" Many fortunate individuals ranked high for that position, but last place went to politicians.
- Napoleon was known to suffer from aelurophobia—the fear of cats.

- "If you don't want to work, you have to work to earn enough money so that you won't have to work." – *Ogden Nash*
- Thanksgiving Day wasn't an official holiday until 1863, 242 years after the Pilgrims' first Thanksgiving "feast." The custom of eating turkey for dinner on this holiday was established largely by the poultry industry after World War II, not by any evidence that this was the Pilgrims' first Thanksgiving meal.
- The number 1, followed by 100 zeros, is a googol. The Australian slang for a fool or simpleton is a "goog."
- When one minister telephones another minister long-distance, he has placed a parson-to-parson call.

Detailed Data

- More oranges are grown in Brazil than in any other country in the world.
- Mt. Whitney is the highest point in the mainland U.S. at 14,495 feet above sea level. Only 86 miles away in the same California county, lies the lowest point, Death Valley, at 276 feet below sea level.
- An attractive, very young model was accused of marrying an ill octogenarian (who happened to own several large expensive homes) just for his money. "Oh, no," she defended herself, "I love him for his charming manors."
- "It is the chiefest point of happiness that a man be willing to be what he is." – *D. Erasmu*
- At some places in Antarctica, the ice cap is more than three miles thick.
- The odds of winning a Bingo game on the first five numbers called are 1,700,000 to 1.
- During its first 40 years of production, 80 million games of *Monopoly* were sold.
- Ginger ale was developed about 1850 in Ireland. Canada Dry wasn't on the U.S. market until 1921.
- "To quit smoking is the easiest thing I ever did; I ought to know because I've done it hundreds of times."– *Mark Twain*
- Some of America's famous folks who were also pharmacists

include Hubert Humphrey, O. Henry, Benjamin Franklin, and Benedict Arnold.

- Typists everywhere owe a debt to Bette Nesmith Graham who was the person responsible for the invention of Liquid Paper in 1951. Homeowners will also be glad to know that Liquid Paper can be used to mask stains in tile grout.

- Although scientist Clarence Birdseye is called the "Father of Frozen Foods," he continually gave the credit to the Eskimos, to whom preservation by freezing was nothing new. Birdseye earned money for college by trapping rats and selling them to a geneticist.

- A less-than-intelligent would-be bank robber handed a teller a note in a Queens, New York bank that instructed her to hand over "all your tens, twenties, and thirties." He then had the gumption to hole up in a motel only one block from the bank where he was apprehended a very short time later.

More Awesome Facts

- In the early 1900s, before the advent of the automobile, Chicago's streets were cleared of 600,000 tons of manure each year.

- The word *graffiti* comes from the Italian word for "scratching."

- It was Theodore Roosevelt who came up with the expression "tossing one's hat into the ring," when he entered the 1912 race for the presidency. "Eating one's hat" was first used by Charles Dickens in *Pickwick Papers*. To "don" one's hat is a contraction of "do on," and to "doff" one's hat is the shortening of "do off."

Jefferson's unknown contribution

- Thomas Jefferson introduced pasta to America when he returned from a trip to France, bringing home a machine that made spaghetti.

- The Great Wall of China is 4,600 miles long and 25 feet

high. It is believed that construction began around 400 BC, continuing sporadically until the 1600s.

- Gophers dig tunnels up to 800 feet long.
- Antonio Stradivari made his famous violins in the late 1600s. The violin has the highest pitch of the stringed instruments. Non-musical folks who travel a lot might refer to a violin as a very bad hotel.
- The neutral country of Switzerland has not been at war since 1515.
- In Argentina, an 8-year-old boy managed to steal a school bus, steer it through three levels of a parking garage, and drive it out into traffic. It seems he had been offered $13 to complete this feat.
- A yarmulke is the skullcap worn by Jewish men for prayer and special ceremonies. A New Orleans boutique, DuSay's, offers white yarmulkes, decorated with a blue Star of David. For dogs, it sells for around $2.98 and features a chinstrap to secure the skullcap to Fido's head.
- Our synonym for jacket, "blazer," takes its name from the style of jacket worn by all the officers of a certain British ship, *The Blazer*.
- "By others' faults, wise men correct their own."

  – Noah Webster
- Baby boys are dressed in blue and baby girls in pink. This is because superstitious folks in the old days believed that evil spirits hanging around the crib could be driven away by certain colors. Blue was considered a very strong color, and because boys were esteemed above girls in ancient times, boys were dressed in blue. Legend has it that girls were born inside pink roses, hence their clothing color of pink.
- A veto gives the president the power to kill a law that has already passed through the legislative branch. The word *veto* is a Latin word, and it means "I forbid."
- Why do people say that worrying can give you an ulcer? An ulcer can be formed when digestive juices eat through the stomach lining. The juices contain acid. Acid production is

stimulated by stress and tobacco use, speeding up the breakdown of the tissue.

Did You Know?

- Why is Los Angeles' basketball team called the L.A. Lakers? Because the team's original home was Minneapolis, Minnesota, the "Land of 10,000 Lakes." The team took the name with them when they moved to L.A. in 1960.
- It's estimated that 50 percent of all famous athletes' autographs on the market are forgeries.
- In 1856, Anthony Gaussardia became the first American to receive a patent for the embalming process, the method of replacing the body fluids of a corpse with chemicals.
- "The Star-Spangled Banner" was not officially declared America's national anthem until 1931. Prior to that, it was just a popular patriotic song. The famous poem written by Washington lawyer Francis Scott Key during the War of 1812 was set to the tune of a popular English drinking song.
- About one-fifth of the world's population lives in China.
- The first singing telegram was delivered in 1933.

Final Facts

- Thomas Edison was once asked if he exercised, to which he replied, "I use my body just to carry my brain around."
- Be warned against stealing kisses from unsuspecting maidens. A certain Frenchman tried it on the city streets, and the mademoiselle promptly bit off his tongue in self-defense.
- "Anybody who watches three games of football in a row should be declared brain dead."   – *Erma Bombeck*
- The British invented the modern-day paper clip around 1900.
- If you are an expert on the subject of brolliology, then you know everything there is to know about umbrellas. "Brolly" is the British term for umbrella, an item that dates back to ancient Egypt.
- Those with expensive tastes nibble on caviar, which is nothing more than the eggs of the Acipenseidae species of fish, the largest of which is the Beluga. The eggs are strained through a sieve to remove the eggs' membranes, then soaked in brine.

It takes only 15 minutes to make caviar. An old Italian proverb testifies, "Who eats caviar eats flies, dung, and salt."

- What does the bacterial food poisoning salmonella have to do with salmon? Actually, nothing. The name is attributed to Daniel Salmon, an American pathologist who died in 1914.

- At a racetrack near Pittsburgh, the deadline to place bets in the 7th race was drawing near. The date was 7/7/77, and gamblers were flocking to place their money on the 7th horse. Shortly before time was up, lightning zig-zagged across the sky, striking and destroying the tote board. Those superstitious folks who withdrew their wagers following this bolt from heaven weren't smiling after the race ... the horse won.

- Leprosy is caused by a bacteria that is about 1/4000th of an inch long. It became known as Hansen's Disease in 1874 when a Norwegian physician of that name discovered the bacteria. Although leprosy is contagious, not very many people exposed to it actually get the disease. It mainly occurs in warm climates, and there are believed to be between 10 and 15 million cases in the world, with only 4,000 of those in the United States.

13

UNIDENTIFIED FLYING OBJECTS DO THEY EXIST?—YOU DECIDE

By Mona Lee McKown

Close Encounters of the Third Kind

- A "close encounter of the third kind" is terminology used for an alleged encounter between humans and visitors from outer space.

- In Pascagoula, Mississippi, Charlie Hickson, who was 42 at the time, and his 19-year-old friend Calvin Parker were doing some night fishing when they encountered extraterrestrials. As the men were fishing, a huge, bright-blue object, shaped like a fish, hovered a few yards away. Three small, wrinkled beings approached the two men. The beings had claw-like hands and pointed ears. The young Calvin fainted from the shock, and Charlie was taken onto the alien craft. Charlie remembers that the aliens did not touch him; he was just "floating." After entering the space craft, he was placed in front of a large instrument that looked like an eye. After the examination was over he "floated" back to where he had been fishing, rejoining the unconscious Calvin. After the incident, Calvin and Charlie reported their experience to the sheriff's office and told their story. Dr. James Harder of the University of California was later called in to hypnotize the two men, in hopes of finding out more information about what actually happened. Dr. Harder found that Calvin and Charlie were not crackpots and that something "not of this earth" did appear on the night of October 11, 1973, in Mississippi.

Sighting by the Famous

- In October, 1973 the former U.S. President, Jimmy Carter, who was at the time governor of Georgia, filed a report of a UFO sighting. He was standing outside in Leary, Georgia, on January 6, 1969, at about 7:15 P.M., waiting to speak to the local Lions Club when he and several other people spotted a light which was as bright as the moon, but somewhat smaller, about 30 degrees above the horizon. The light moved closer and then farther away several times before it finally disappeared.

Close Encounters of the Fourth Kind

- Encounters under this category usually contain some type of personal contact, such as an abduction into an alien vessel.
- In Brazil on October 15, 1957, a 23-year-old farmer was tilling his field with his tractor when a "luminous egg-shaped object" about 35 feet long and 23 feet wide hovered over him and landed close by. Antonio Villa Boas said his tractor engine died, and the lights went off. Four beings came out of the vessel and dragged him into the craft. There were five other humanoids in the craft. Villas Boas was stripped of his clothes, and his captors took blood from his chin, but he said he felt "no pain or prickling." After the examination by the beings, a beautiful woman entered and seduced him. Villas Boas figured he may have ended up being the father of an extraterrestrial child. After he was returned to his tractor, he watched the UFO rise slowly and turn slightly. It then shot off like a bullet. About four months later, Villa Boas went to the doctor because he was not feeling well. After the examination, Dr. Olavo Fontes concluded that Villa Boas was probably suffering from a case of "radiation poisoning."

Food from the Stars

- Eagle River, Wisconsin was visited by a UFO on April 18, 1961. Joe Simonton, a master plumber in Eagle River, was the recipient of four "pancakes" from the occupants of the

UFO. When Joe saw the craft, he approached it. A hatch opened up, and he saw three "men" inside. One of them handed Joe a silver-colored jug and motioned that he wanted some water. After Joe filled the container with water and handed it back to the beings, he noticed that one of them was cooking on some type of flameless stove. He motioned to the cook that he would like to have one of the "pancakes." It was then that one of the occupants picked up four pancake-like objects and handed them to Simonton. Afterwards, the craft took off, leaving Joe with his new food. He said he then ate one, and it tasted like cardboard. He kept one

Food from Space

What, no Syrup!

of the "pancakes" and gave the other two to various UFO investigation agencies. The group from Northwestern University checked out the ingredients of the "pancake" and said it contained "flour, sugar and grease."

Hello! Is Anybody Home?

- Astronomers are convinced that somebody is out there. Scientists believe that there are intelligent beings from far-off civilizations trying to communicate with us. When radio telescopes first picked up mysteriously regular signals from deep space, a number of scientists thought communication was actually happening. However, it turned out to be pulsars, gigantic collapsing stars, that were and are emitting the strange radio patterns.

- When the *Pioneer 10* spacecraft was sent off to investigate our solar system and others as well, a special message was engraved on the side of the ship, in hope of communicating with other life-forms. NASA scientists engraved a stylized picture of a man and a woman with their right hands raised, in what it is hoped is a gesture of greeting and peace. Other engraved symbols tell the extraterrestrials where we are so they can write back or pay us a visit.

- Others have also left messages engraved on spacecraft for aliens to find. Bruce Montgomery worked for the Jet Propulsion Laboratory as an engineer and sneaked a personal message on the two *Voyager* spacecraft launched in 1977. He placed his coded message on a valve package plate that he had designed. He stamped "DEI/FEIF" on the plate. This coded message came from an inside joke at Cal Tech where Montgomery had gone to school. The DEI stands for "Dabney Eats It," which was the unofficial motto of an undergraduate residence's food service. FEIF is "Fleming Eats It Faster," another description of the dining hall's food.

- In the 1870s, a Frenchman named Charles Cros tried to persuade the French government to construct a huge magnifying glass that would focus the sun's rays on Mars. The lens would then be manipulated slightly to burn letters into the planet's surface, forming sentences.

- One of the most innovative mathematicians of all time, Karl Friedrich Gauss, proposed that hundreds of square miles in the Siberian steppes should be planted with long lines of pine trees. These pine trees would be symbolic representations of the Pythagorean theorem. Gauss believed this distinctive pattern would communicate to beings on other planets that the beings on this planet were creatures of intelligence and would be worthy of a visit. Gauss died in 1855 without seeing his idea implemented.

A Multitude of Sightings

- One of the first written accounts of a UFO sighting was found on an Egyptian papyrus which was part of the annals of Thutmose III, who reigned around 1504-1450 BC. This recorded sighting is therefore 3,400 years old.

- During the 4th century AD, when the Roman author Julius Obsequens was believed to have lived, he recorded many unusual phenomena, some of which could be interrupted as UFO sightings. Here are a few examples of his writings: (216

BC) Things like ships were seen in the sky over Italy.... At Arpi (180 Roman miles east of Rome in Apulia) a round shield was seen in the sky. ... At Capua, the sky was all on fire, and one saw figures like ships...(90 BC). In the territory of Spoletium (65 Roman miles north of Rome in Umbria), a globe of fire, of golden color, fell to the earth, gyrating. It then seemed to increase in size, rose from the earth, and ascended into the sky where it obscured the disc of the sun with its brilliance. It revolved towards the eastern quadrant of the sky.

- UFO sightings were also recorded during the 12th, 14th and 15th centuries in Europe.
- In 1896 and 1897, there were dozens of reports of strange flying lights and barrel-shaped "airships." These reports appeared in U.S. and Canadian newspapers. These reports precede by several years any documented flights of airplanes.
- Professor David Saunders of the psychology department of the University of Chicago claims that abnormally large numbers of UFO sightings occur every 61 months.

It Happened One Night

- During the month of November in 1957, the Air Force acknowledged 414 reports of UFO sightings. The first sighting during that time happened in Levelland, Texas. It all began with a report phoned in by a farm worker who said he had just had a torpedo-shaped ball of flame follow him while he was driving his truck along Route 116. He said as the object came closer to his truck the truck quit, and the lights went out. He then jumped out of his truck and fell to the ground as the object roared over his head. He said it was so close that he could feel the heat. A.J. Fowler was the patrolman running the telephones that night. With this first call he didn't really put much stock in the report. However, soon the phone began ringing off the hook with similar calls. In the next three hours, there were close to two dozen calls about this enormous egg-shaped light that caused vehicles to stop and lights to go out.

There Was a Reward

- A reward was offered by Cutty Sark, the whiskey manufacturer, for the capture of a spaceship or other vehicle which could be verified by the Science Museum of London as actually coming from outer space. A million British pounds were offered as the reward. The British Unidentified Flying Object Research Association rated the chance of someone's actually collecting as nil.

Investigators of UFOs

- In 1948 the U.S. Air Force created Project Sign which began the official documentation of UFOs. The next year the project was reorganized into Project Grudge and then into Project Blue Book. The purpose of Project Blue Book was to investigate and evaluate UFO reports within the United States and in other countries where there may have been a potential threat to our national security, whether that threat was from foreign powers or from outer space. The project was quite effective during its 18 years of work. There were more than 12,600 reported cases in its files. Most of these cases were explained as natural phenomena although 701 cases did remain unidentified.

UFOs...Do You Believe?

- In December of 1975, in three separate counties in Florida, several police officers sighted an amazing, technicolor UFO three stories high and at least as long as three football fields. The Federal Aviation Administration could not come up with an explanation for the rainbow-colored spacecraft. Several witnesses said that they saw it land in a wooded area and then take off again.

- The sightings of UFOs have been happening for a very long time. On an island in Hunan province, China, a carving depicting cylindrical objects resembling spacecraft, with what might be their extraterrestrial occupants, was dated at about 47,000 years. This date put the sighting within the time-span of Neanderthal Man.

Their Reality is Predicted

- Maris de Long, a present-day psychic, predicts that before the year 2000 there will be more UFO sightings reported, and it will be discovered that UFOs do exist. Maris also predicts that the extraterrestrial life forms will migrate to earth because their own planet is burning up with radiation. It will also be discovered that there are already several thousand of them living with us.

- It has been predicted that by the year 2000 UFOs will give us the knowledge to harness the sun's energy. This event will bring together the top scientists of the world, which will benefit all of mankind.

- Kebrina Kinkade has several predictions dealing with UFOs. She believes that we will join forces with Russia in space travel after contact is made with a UFO. We will also discover several life-bearing planets outside our solar system. Kinkade also predicts that it will be proven that the Bermuda Triangle is the center of UFO activity. She predicts that these things will happen by the year 2000.

The Last Look

- To many people, UFOs are a harmless hoax. Yet, there have been so many reported sightings by so many people from different walks of life and from different parts of the world that we have to wonder what the reality is. The sightings have been explained away as natural occurrences, whether it be meteorites, weather balloons, unusual cloud formations or practical jokes, but there still remain those few cases which have never been explained by any of these possibilities. The most realistic way of thinking is that we are faced with a series of strange, inexplicable phenomena. Maybe tomorrow the truth will be found, but for now we simply are left to wonder.

A Final Fact

- Statistically, UFO sightings are at their greatest number during those times when Mars is closest to Earth.

14

HOBBIES

By J.C. Walker

Mighty Mites

- Mention "hobbies," and it's likely you'll get a response about one of the most avidly pursued pastimes today—that of radio-controlled "big boys' toys"—miniature boats, airplanes, motorcycles, helicopters, and gliders. They come in a variety as enormous as the real things, and their operators are among the most rabid in the hobby world. The "Flying Tigers," for example, are groups across the country organized to pursue their hobby love—flying tiny prop airplanes that perform mid-air aerobatics as breathtaking as any done by the big guys.

- This fascination with teeny-weeny vehicles isn't really a new thing, either. A group in Dundee, Scotland—fittingly known as the Dundee Model Boat Club—boasts that it has been in existence since "the 20th April 1885 at the Coffee House, Candle Lane, Dundee for the 'furtherance of the recreation of all aspects of Model Boating.'" This, of course, started out as a miniature yachting club, and there was a considerable to-do in the 1960s when some young upstarts began using radio-controlled power boats, much to the chagrin of the traditionalists.

- And if you've always fantasized about owning an actual Harley-Davidson motorcycle, here's a chance to do so without raising the eyebrows of your mother-in-law or your boss. The venerable company has licensed a model manufacturer to produce 1/12-sized plastic copies available for the "intermediate to advanced builder" of models. While, of course, you can't actually move the bikes around like the radio-controlled goodies, you can certainly picture yourself roaring down the highway on your Electra Glide or Fat Boy FLSTF, considerable bargains over the real thing at $49.50.

Life Isn't Fair

• "The Olympic commentators tell us that the gold medal winners have trained for this all their lives. They've worked 12 hours a day, seven days a week, for months on end. Of course, so did the losers."
– Linda Perret

Does This Really Sound Like Fun to You?

• For some people, work is play. The Ironman Triathlon World Championship held every autumn in Hawaii is a good example. The outing consists of a 2.4-mile swim, followed by the 112-mile bike race and wrapped up by a 26.2-mile run, completed the same day. One of the competitors, Governor Gary Johnson of New Mexico, said before the event, "At best I'm going to be mid-pack (among 1,500 entrants), but this is the best in the world."

Out of Touch

• If you're searching for a new hobby that's definitely out of the ordinary, consider joining the 2,000 enthusiasts who collect antique telephone insulators. Really. The interest now boasts annual conventions, magazines and brokers, and is considered to be among the fastest-growing hobbies in the country. For the uninitiated, telephone insulators are cone-shaped glass or porcelain caps that protected connections on phone lines in the days before fiber optics and underground

Need A Hobby?

TELEPHONE INSULATOR CONVENTION

Last Warning
Stay outside
the ropes.

SH

systems. They come in a variety of colors ranging from deep blue to bright aqua, depending on the quality of the glass used to make them during their 100-year history. While you could order (if you wanted to) 1,000 No. 9 Pony Insulators for $38.70 in 1909, you would pay far more than that today for one outstanding "jewel" from a professional telephone insulator collector. You can find insulators available for sale at conventions, in classified ads in magazines, and on numerous Internet sites, where one insulator enthusiast exclaimed, "Not much can top a good insulator show!"

Leap of Faith

- Bungee jumping seems to be on the downswing, as it were, since its pinnacle of popularity in about 1992, but that doesn't mean the thrill of jumping head first off a sheer precipice has diminished for many fans—we're all familiar now with the sight of young men who propel themselves from any handy cliff face, hot air balloon, crane top or even helicopter and, hopefully, bounce back. Anthropologists believe the insanity was first practiced on Pentecost Island in the South Pacific by natives who would leap from bamboo scaffolding several hundred feet high as a rite of passage into manhood. Apparently, the trick was to use a piece of vine that was shorter than the tower to tie around the ankles, although the real test of manhood was that nobody measured the vine.

Street Smarts?

- You might want to consider the relatively new sport of street luge. Yes, it's true. The Olympic sport of barreling down an ice chute while reclining feet first on a vehicle no bigger than a child's sled has been adapted to city streets with the obvious disadvantages of rocky surfaces, oil slicks and sandy spots. Participants frequently reach speeds of 80 mph and even more frequently end up crashing into curbs, trees and signposts. One avid enthusiast, who is promoting the sport, was recently interviewed while nursing a "bruised, possibly broken tailbone and a shredded ankle," and he talked about the thrill he gets while speeding downhill. Jarrett "Dr. GoFast" Ewanek has raced in street luge competition for 10 years, and set the world speed limit at the ESPN 1997 Extreme

Games. "The thrill and rush is only a part of it," he said. "The real appeal to me is coming up with a concept for a piece of racing equipment, spending time optimizing the design, and then building the device to take me or any other racers that use my gear to victory." The aeronautical engineer also says his favorite color is "blurred pavement."

Tally Ho, Dude

- The sport of bike polo has been around for a long time, but it's only recently begun to grow in popular appeal, especially, of course, in California. The rules and equipment are pretty much as you would expect, although the aristocratic appeal of polo played on horses seems to be lacking. It's believed the game was invented more than 100 years ago in India when British soldiers used bicycles to save wear and tear on their equine partners while practicing polo skills. It may sound like a simple and straightforward game to play, but really accomplished bike poloists perfect their technique in dribbling the ball parallel to the sidelines and fooling opponents by hitting it between the wheels of their own bikes.

Icy Determination

- Rock climbing has gotten too tame for many of its fans, and they've discovered a great new way to get that old thrill while hanging by a thin line hundreds of feet off the ground. Climbers are now lining up for waterfall ice climbing at such sites as Bridal Veil Falls and Ames Ice Hose near Ophir, Colorado.

All Dolled Up

- And then, of course, there are the collectors. Collections of children's toys, games, vehicles and pastimes have grown enormously in recent years, and a stroll through a doll collectors' convention will convince you that this is not kid stuff. A Madame Alexander "Wicked Stepmother" interpretation from Disney's *Snow White* can be had in all her evil splendor for a cool $299.95, while the Mattel 50th Anniversary commemorative Barbie is available for only $625.00. For nostalgia buffs, there's the "I Love Lucy" doll, with the famous redheaded ditz outfitted in polka dot puffery, again at $299.95. Traditionalists would probably be more interested in the 21-inch antique Kestner doll made in about 1880 which features a "pink Ked body, sleep eyes, and human hair" and a price tag of $900.

Balancing Act

- For many people, the enjoyment of their hobbies comes from the companionship of others with similar interests. One group that trains and showcases jugglers has been operating for well over 22 years out of a lobby in a building at MIT. Individual members have come and gone, but every Sunday for five or six hours up to 20 jugglers meet in Lobby 10 to share ideas, tricks and suggestions. Like AA, all members refer to each other only by first names, although occasionally additional monikers (like "the Amazing Philbert") will creep in. Members of the group believe it is the oldest in the world, and it attracts jugglers from nearby states and communities as well as a few MIT students. Appropriately, a few of those students have noted that there is a correlation between mathematical ability and juggling, since descriptions of juggling throws are made in mathematical terms. One participant who calls herself "the juggler formerly known as Pauline" states proudly that nothing in the lobby has been broken by the group in more than 10 years, although they do sometimes have to stack nearby furniture and tables to retrieve clubs that have become entangled mid-air with chandeliers.

You Really Need to Get Out More

- Site recently discovered on a cruise of the Internet: a collection of pictures of their satellite dishes submitted by fans of "Dish of the Week."

Just a Couple of Swingers

- An enterprising engineering firm in New Zealand saw early on that simply providing bungee jumps would severely limit their market, so the engineers set about in 1995 to provide what they call the Ultimate Swing. Now, promoted with a picture of a smiling gray-haired couple about to embark on the greatest adventure of their marriage, the Ultimate Swing is "a giant 50-meter plunging swoop down over the Aerobe River, launching from the bungee platform and suspended from a cable high above, spanning the gorge." Promoters claim the swing is now four times more popular than the bungee jump.

Wash Out

- Sand sculpting hobbyists set a world's record in September 1997 when they built the largest and tallest sand city in history on a stretch of isolated beach on San Diego's Mission Bay. Towering mythical sea creatures plunged out of rough seas; aquatic lions and dolphins stood guard, and King Neptune kept watch from his high point in an underseas castle. The creation—estimated to have been 480 feet long and up to 64 feet tall—was possible because of the "magic potion" the sculptors used, a concoction of water and Elmer's Glue applied by spray bottle. Even though this gave the piece a rock-hard appearance, in reality, a heavy downpour or high winds would have been enough to undo it. The sculpture couldn't help but attract attention—promoters charged a $5 admission to view the city, and Bill Gates of Microsoft fame held a company party there for 6,000 of his closest friends, complete with music, dancing, fireworks, and a light show. Within several weeks after the event, though, the city of Atlantis was again lost when ocean tides reclaimed the beach and the sculptors' creation.

Huzzah!

- If the Computer Age is becoming just too much for you to handle, consider a full-fledged membership in the Society for Creative Anachronism. This is the group that has created "an alternative reality" by staging weekend medieval retreats, featuring jousts, armed battles, and battle-ax throwing competitions, all in European dress and language of the pre-1700s, of course. Less well-known activities include archery, leatherwork, heraldry, calligraphy, music, dancing, brewing, spinning and weaving. The SCA was born in 1966 in Berkeley, California, when a backyard medieval fair was deemed a roaring success enjoyed by all, and the group now claims more than 25,000 members across the country which has been divided into 13 Kingdoms containing smaller fiefdoms and baronies. There are also branches in Europe, Japan, and Australia.

- While membership is fully expected to walk, talk and dress in a medieval way, administrative members admit it's "the past as we would like it to be," without starving peasants and that pesky Black Plague. The SCA's newcomer sheet advises new members to prepare for a weekend get-together by bringing feast and everyday garb, feast gear, armor and weapons, as well as cellular phones, sunglasses, cassettes and stereos, bug repellent, and cameras.

Leap of Faith

- Two California brothers might be considered the Kings of Bungee. John and Peter Kockelman both have degrees in engineering from California Polytechnic State University, and they put those skills to good use in furthering the cause in American society. They estimate they have rigged more than 50,000 jumps during their careers, and they have each set a world record for longest bungee jump. They designed the bungee cord for the now-famous GMC truck commercial and wrote a computer program that tracks the distance, velocity, acceleration, air-drag and force of the jumper at any time in the bouncing cycle. NASA has hired the brothers to computer-model a moon landing bungee jump to simulate zero gravity. They head the largest U.S. supplier of cords to the bungee industry, and Peter and John estimate that of their 50,000 jumps, 35,000 were from cranes, 10,000 from bridges and 5,000 from balloons. Their jump repertoire also includes leaps from hang-gliders, parachutes, helicopters, redwood trees, sports coliseums and hotel lobbies. Fittingly, the two have also authored the *North American Bungee Association Safety Standards*.

15

"WELL, WHAT DO YA KNOW?"
by Kathy Wolfe

Wart You Lookin' At?

- Can you get a wart from touching the skin of a toad? Absolutely not. A wart is caused from infection by one of 30 different viruses.

It's Enough to Drive You to Think

- Nearly 2,400 million gallons of Coca-Cola Classic were consumed in 1992.
- Paul Revere was a noted silversmith and copper plater. He also crafted dentures from ivory and gold.
- LeRoy Ripley, the creator of "Believe It Or Not," originally considered titling his newspaper column "Champs or Chumps," because his original news feature contained sports oddities. He later expanded it to include all sorts of weird happenings.
- The human hand contains 27 bones. Famous left-handers include Leonardo daVinci, Jack the Ripper, Babe Ruth, and Harry S. Truman.
- "The only place where success comes before work is in a dictionary." – *Vidal Sassoon*
- Some folks suffer from "arachibutyrophobia," which is the fear of peanut butter sticking to the roof of your mouth.
- President Lyndon Johnson spent $62,000 on the 1967 wedding of his daughter Lynda to Charles Robb.
- Austrian immigrant John Hertz ran away from home at age 11, and was a delivery man, a boxer, a sportswriter, a salesman, and founder of the Yellow Cab Company before

beginning the Hertz Drive-Ur-Self System, later Hertz Rent-A-Car.

- A pharmacist came up with a scale to rank peppers from mildest to hottest. Bell peppers' score was at the bottom with zero, with habaneros peppers scorching off the top between 200,000 and 300,000.

Chew on That for a Minute

- Sam Benedict was dining at the Waldorf-Astoria Hotel in New York City one evening when he asked the chef to prepare a dish he had concocted in his mind. It consisted of poached eggs, a slice of ham, and an English muffin, all topped with hollandaise sauce. His dish was thereafter referred to as Eggs Benedict.

It'll Bring Tears to Your Eyes

- A woman's heart beats faster than a man's, averaging 80 beats per minute compared to 72 beats for men. Yet, a woman's metabolism—the process of turning food into energy—is usually lower than a man's.
- In the 1936 Olympics held in Berlin, the crowd in the stands began screaming that Stella Walsh, the winner of the women's 100-meter dash, was really a man. Under pressure from the crowd, the Olympic officials compelled Ms. Walsh to disrobe in front of the crowd.
- The average American male cries 1.5 times per month. You can catch the average female crying more than 5 times per month.

Tax Your Patience

- The lifetime of the average pencil is about 50,000 words.
- About one-third of all Americans mail in their tax return on April 15.

Make You Shudder

- There were more fatalities from the flu during World War I than there were from battle casualties.
- It would take only 60 seconds for a lightly clothed person to freeze to death in Antarctica.

And Zap Your Apple-tite

- It is the general assumption of many that the forbidden fruit eaten by Adam and Eve in the Garden of Eden was an apple. The Bible does not mention the word *apple*, but refers only to "the fruit from the tree that is in the middle of the garden." The sacred book of the Moslems, the *Koran*, states that it was a banana.
- The specialties of a certain eating establishment include SPAM nachos and SPAM in cream sauce. Recipes for SPAM Cheesecake and SPAM Mousse were the winners in a 1992 recipe contest.
- An old, folk remedy reported to cure stammering involved slapping the face of the person with a piece of raw liver.

Come On, Gear Up For More

- In 1974, the funeral of His Most Gracious Majesty the Lord Grimsley of Katmandu was held, and what an occasion it was. His body lay in state for three weeks, as the corpse rested on an elegant bed of silk. One thousand carnations adorned his casket. His favorite poetry was read at the service. Pretty fancy fare for a parrot.
- A "previously recounted humorous narrative" is, in simpler terms, an old joke.
- In 1900, the most popular names for babies were John and Mary.
- In an attempt to commit suicide, a certain gentleman set himself on fire. At the last minute, he changed his mind, dropped to the ground, and rolled, endeavoring to put out the flames. Unfortunately, he rolled right off a cliff, and his suicide attempt was successful.
- The "politically correct" term for *clumsy* is "uniquely coordinated."
- In 1900, a European gentleman spent 55 days traveling from Vienna to Paris. Nothing so unusual about that, except that he journeyed this 871 miles while walking on his hands.
- "A fanatic is one who can't change his mind and won't change the subject."   *– Sir Winston Churchill*

- About 7.5 million people live in New York City.
- Author Lee Ezell published a book called *What Men Understand About Women*. A quick look inside the front cover reveals nothing but blank pages.
- If your children inform you they're heading over to the natatorium, where are they going? Why, to the swimming pool, of course!
- The celebrity who still holds his long-standing record for the most fan mail, numbering hundreds of millions of letters, is Mickey Mouse.
- The driest of all 50 U.S. states is Nevada. Average yearly precipitation is 9 inches. The word *Nevada* is the Spanish word for "snow-clad." Eighty percent of the land in Nevada is owned by the federal government.

Think About This

- A certain gentleman had his will drawn up and left all his worldly goods to his wife, but only if she remarried. He gave his reason as this, "Then, there will be at least one man to regret my death."

Breathe In, Breathe Out

- Although Chicago has long been referred to as the "Windy City," the windiest city in the United States is actually Great Falls, Montana, where wind speeds average 13.1 mph. Chicago is well down the line at Number 16. It wasn't the gusts blowing across Lake Michigan that gave the city its name anyway. They helped reinforce the nickname given by a New York City newspaper editor at the 1893 Chicago World's Fair. There was so much bragging being done by the people of Chicago about the fair, the editor branded them the "Windy City."
- If you are a lepidopterist, your hobby is collecting moths and butterflies. If piscatology is your bag, then you're a fine fisherman.
- When driving in Britain, be sure you use your "self-canceling trafficator" regularly. That is to say, your turn signal.
- If you know someone employed as a "hot walker," he works

at the racetrack. He's the guy who walks the horses around after a strenuous practice or race.

- Calvin Coolidge, the first president to be born on the Fourth of July, was given the nickname "genius for inactivity." This shy, closemouthed gentleman slept 10 hours a night and enjoyed playing practical jokes.
- "Prosperity is only an instrument to be used, not a deity to be worshiped."   – *Calvin Coolidge*
- When you're told to "fish or cut bait," you're being admonished to make yourself useful.
- A blue whale caught near Argentina weighed nearly 200 tons, about equal to the weight of 30 African elephants. The babies of this species gain about 200 pounds a day during their first year of life.

Keep Going

- Sigmund Freud's hobby was collecting mushrooms.
- If someone comes at you with a "Branock device," don't be alarmed. He's just trying to measure your shoe size.
- Why are potatoes called "spuds"? Just because the sharp spade used to dig them up is called a spud.
- The Pontiac GTO was a popular car in the '60s and '70s, but what did the letters "GTO" stand for? The abbreviation meant Gran Turismo Omologato, which translates to "Grand Award Sedan."
- The average person sweats about a quart of liquid each day.

Come On, Gear Up For More

- At Mt. Waialeale in Kauai, Hawaii, it rains about 350 days a year.
- Zane Grey, author of more than 50 Wild West novels, was given the name Pearl at birth. Perhaps, it was his birthplace of Zanesville, Ohio, that this former dentist took for his pseudonym.
- If you stay someplace that is stylish and classy, it is said to be "ritzy." This is thanks to a Swiss gentleman named Cesar Ritz, the 13th child of a poor farmer and his wife. Due to finances, Cesar was forced to go to work as a waiter. He was

fired by three different hotels before finally getting the hang of the hotel business. At age 38, he opened his own hotel in Paris. A former mansion, elegantly furnished, made his name synonymous with excellence.

- A study was conducted to examine the effect of your name on your life. The exact same essays written by grade-school children were turned in to teachers. Three of the essays were submitted by Karen, Lisa, and David. The names Elmer, Bertha, and Hubert headed up the other same three essays. Karen, Lisa, and David consistently scored higher on the identical papers.

What's In A Name?

You Made It

- If you are a 160-pound person, your body contains about five quarts of blood. Unless, of course, you live at a high altitude, where your body could contain up to two quarts more than that of a person living at low altitudes. Since there is less oxygen in higher altitudes, the additional blood is needed to carry extra oxygen to the body cells.
- A French acrobat named Charles Blondin strung a 1,300-foot-long rope across Niagara Falls in 1859. He not only walked across it, he also did so with his hands and feet tied. Just to make it interesting, he made part of the trip on stilts, then switched to a gunnysack.
- Ralph Lifshitz loved clothes and had impeccable taste in them. Wanting to break into the world of fashion design, he started working for a necktie company, and designed five-inch-wide ties out of unusual fabrics. They became an instant hit, and Lifshitz, also known as Ralph Lauren, was on his way to his present sales of over $1 billion annually.

What's for Supper?

- The favorite sandwich of the late Vice-President Hubert Humphrey consisted of "peanut butter, bologna, cheddar cheese, lettuce, and mayonnaise on toasted bread with lots of catsup on the side."
- "The Nutcracker" composer and musical genius Peter Tchaikovsky died from drinking water that was infested with cholera.
- If you're served appetizers while visiting Alaska, try the Muktuk. It's an Eskimo recipe consisting of whale skin topped with whale blubber. Dessert in Tanzania might be white-ant pie.
- The 1930s jazz duo of sisters Daisy and Violet Hilton became very popular and wealthy as they toured the East Coast. Daisy was a saxophonist and Violet, her piano accompanist. They were not your ordinary musical group, since they were Siamese twins who were joined at the hip. Unfortunately, their popularity didn't last, and they spent their final years working in the produce department at the grocery store.

Now You Know

- There are about 100,000 miles of blood vessels in the human body.
- A queen bee is only two days old when she is chosen to lead the colony. The queen bee's only job is laying eggs. She lays about 2,000 eggs per day, one every 43 seconds. The worker bees are females; the drones, male. An average colony contains about 50,000 bees.
- "Flattery is like soap... 90% lye."   *– Anonymous*
- Henry Ford kept a framed photograph of Adolph Hitler on his desk.
- The genius behind the Porsche automobile was also the designer of the Volkswagen Beetle. The first vehicle designed by Dr. Ferdinand Porsche was actually a tank, developed for the Austrian Army. He never saw an automobile with his own name on it. The Porsche as an automobile was developed by Ferdinand Porsche II, who built the first one out of leftover

16

HOLLYWOOD
By V.B. Darrington

The First Fact

- Hollywood's first Western, *The Great Train Robbery* (1903), was actually filmed in New Jersey.

"Aw Geez, They're Kissing!"

- The first screen kiss came in the film, *The Widow Jones*, in 1896. A reviewer at the time described it as "absolutely disgusting." The first French kiss in a Hollywood film occurred in *Splendor in the Grass* (1961), between Natalie Wood and Warren Beatty.

- The longest kiss recorded on film occurs between Cary Grant and Ingrid Bergman in Alfred Hitchcock's *Notorious* (1946).

"Hot" Feet

- Actors and actresses aren't the only ones to make their mark in the famed cement of Graumann's Chinese Theatre in Hollywood. Three famous horses made their hoof prints: Champion (Gene Autry's horse), Tony (Tom Mix's horse), and Trigger (Roy Rogers' horse).

WIZ Bits

- A pair of Judy Garland's ruby slippers from *The Wizard of Oz* (1939) sold for $165,000 at an auction in 1988. Several pairs of the slippers are still floating around, however. Experts estimate that as many as nine pairs of the famous props were made for Dorothy. One pair was even equipped with felt soles so they wouldn't make too much noise on "the Yellow Brick Road."

- Liza Minnelli, daughter of Judy Garland, married Jack Haley Jr., son of Jack Haley, who played The Tin Man.

"Fishing" For An Oscar

- While shooting *On Golden Pond* (1981), Katherine Hepburn gave a special gift to her co-star Henry Fonda. She gave him a fishing cap that had belonged to the great Spencer Tracy. Fonda liked the hat so much that he integrated it into the movie. The old fishing hat he wears in nearly every scene was owned by a two-time Oscar winner!

The "Citizen"

- In a 1990 poll of film critics and filmmakers, *Citizen Kane* (1941) was voted the greatest film ever made. It is worth noting that *Citizen Kane* was a box office flop when it was first released and that it won only a single Academy Award.
- Steven Speilberg is a great fan of Orson Welles. He enjoyed the Welles' movie *Citizen Kane* (1941) so much that he paid $60,500 for the Rosebud sled used as a prop in the movie.

Hitchcock's Heritage

- Alfred Hitchcock influenced the horror genre with his memorable shower scene in *Psycho* (1960). The famous director didn't skimp on the details either. The notorious scene was made of 70 different camera shots even though it lasts only 45 seconds. Chocolate sauce was used to give the impression of blood.
- Alfred Hitchcock always managed to make a brief appearance in his films. However, for *Lifeboat* (1944), he was faced with a difficult problem—the entire movie was set in a lifeboat out at sea, and there were only a few characters in the boat. His ingenious solution was to place a photograph of himself in a newspaper that one of the characters reads during the course of the film. He can be seen in the "before" portion of a "before" and "after" ad for a diet product.

Fabulous Fakes

- The largest outdoor film set ever built was the Roman Forum used in *The Fall of the Roman Empire* (1964). It was 1,312 feet long by 754 feet wide, took 1,100 workers seven months to construct, and rose some 260 feet in the air.

- The largest indoor film set ever built was the landing site for the UFO in *Close Encounters of the Third Kind* (1977). Constructed inside a 10-million-cubic-foot hangar in Mobile, Alabama, it was 450 feet long by 250 feet wide and was 90 feet tall.
- Windows in movies are often made of clear sugar, especially when an actor is going to jump through one.
- Because they could not find sharks big enough to suit their needs, the producers of *Jaws* (1975) hired a 4-foot-9-inch ex-jockey to stand inside a scaled-down shark cage, thus making the shark look much bigger than it actually was.
- More than 22 million bees were used in *The Swarm* (1978).

"Biggies" Of The Horror Classics

- Bela Lugosi, famous for his role as Dracula, was buried in his character's cloak.
- During close-ups of Bela Lugosi in *Dracula* (1931), flashlights were shone into the actor's eyes to give them an eerie effect.
- One of the reasons Lon Chaney was such an effective silent film star was because he had been raised by deaf-mute parents, thus enhancing his ability to relate emotions and actions without the use of sound.

"The Little Tramp"

- The boots that Charlie Chaplin ate in *The Gold Rush* (1924) were made out of licorice.
- Charlie Chaplin invented his tramp costume with the help of Fatty Arbuckle's pants, Arbuckle's father-in-law's derby, Chester Cockline's cutaway, Ford Sterling's size 14 shoes, and some crepe paper belonging to Mack Swain (which became the tramp's moustache). The only item that belonged to Chaplin was the whangee cane.
- In 1914, Charlie Chaplin made an astounding 35 movies.
- Charlie Chaplin's trademark bowler and cane fetched $150,000 when auctioned.

Bogey & Bacall

- The terrific ending for *Casablanca* was kept a secret through the shoot. Nobody, not even Humphrey Bogart and Ingrid Bergman, knew how the film was going to end until the final scene was ready to be shot.
- Humphrey Bogart was known to cure a hangover by getting drunk all over again. In fact, he formed his own drinking club, The Holmby Hills Rat Pack, which included his wife Lauren Bacall, David Niven, Judy Garland, John Huston, Adlai Stevenson, Peter Lorre, John O'Hara, and Frank Sinatra.
- Lauren Bacall appears to sing in *To Have and Have Not* (1944), but her voice was actually dubbed by none other than Andy Williams!

Re-Takes

- Charlie Chaplin once re-shot a scene in *City Lights* (1931) some 342 times before he felt he had gotten it right. In *Some Like It Hot* (1959), Marilyn Monroe required 59 takes on a scene in which her only line was "Where's the Bourbon?" Similarly, Stanley Kubrick required Shelley Duval to redo a scene 127 times in *The Shining* (1980).

The Unmistakable Voice

- Mel Blanc, the voice of Bugs Bunny and many other beloved cartoon characters, hated carrots. Whenever he was recording the sound track for Bugs, he would keep a bucket next to him where he could spit out the carrots that Bugs was known to eat.

Get The Facts!

- *Indiana Jones and the Last Crusade* (1989) is riddled with mistakes. At the beginning of the film, Indiana Jones crosses the Atlantic by airliner even though it is 1938–one year before the first transatlantic passenger service began. In the airport lounge, two people are reading German newspapers that are dated 1918, 20 years before the year in which the film is set. Finally, the "Republic" of Hatay is ruled by someone referred to as "Your Royal Highness."

- The title says, *Krakatoa, East of Java* (1968), but Krakatoa is really 200 miles west of Java.

Famous Film Scores

- The best-selling record of a song from a film was sung by Bing Crosby in *Holiday Inn* (1942).
- John Williams is the most successful film composer, having written the score for eight of the 10 highest-earning movies in history, *Jaws* (1975), *Star Wars* (1977), *The Empire Strikes Back* (1980), *Raiders of the Lost Ark* (1981), *E.T.*(1982), *Return of the Jedi* (1983), *Indiana Jones and the Temple of Doom* (1984), and *Indiana Jones and the Last Crusade* (1989).

The High Cost Of Insurance

- Fred Astaire's legs were once insured for $1 million. Betty Grable's legs were insured for slightly more—$1.25 million.
- Jimmy Durante once copyrighted his nose. He also had it insured by Lloyd's of London for $100,000.

Banned!

- Prince Rainier has banned all of Grace Kelly's films from being shown in Monaco.
- Iraq banned karate films in 1979.
- Romania banned Mickey Mouse films in 1935 because the animated character was thought to be frightening to children.

Author! Author!

- Tom Wolfe was paid $5 million for the film rights to his novel *Bonfire of the Vanities*, the most ever earned by an author.
- Screenwriter Joe Ezterhas was paid $3 million for his script, *Basic Instinct*, the highest amount ever paid to a screenwriter.
- John Hughes wrote the script for *Weird Science* (1985) in two days. He wrote *The Breakfast Club* (1984) in three days, and *National Lampoon's Vacation* (1983) in four days.
- The screenplay credit for *The Taming of the Shrew* (1929) said, "Written by William Shakespeare. Additional dialogue by Sam Taylor."
- Sherlock Holmes is the most portrayed character on film, having been played by 72 actors in 204 films. The historical

character most represented in films is Napoleon Bonaparte, with 194 film portrayals. Abraham Lincoln is the U.S. president to be portrayed most on film, with 136 films featuring actors playing the role.

- When she performed for the troops during World War II, Marlene Dietrich would entertain the men by playing the musical saw.

- As a token of rebellion, Robert Towne, the famous screen writer, removed his name from the credits of *Greystoke: The Legend of Tarzan, Lord of the Apes.* He was upset by changes that had been made to his script. Instead of his name, he put the name of his Hungarian sheep dog, P.H. Vazak. His dog was later nominated for an Academy Award!

Dog Makes Oscar Debut

- Mae West wrote the majority of her film dialogue.

- Woody Allen originally wanted the title of *Annie Hall* (1977) to be *Anhedonia*, a Greek medical term for someone who can't experience pleasure. Other titles he considered were *Anxiety* and *Annie and Alvy*.

The Last Look

- Two hippopotami were present at the second wedding of Elizabeth Taylor and Richard Burton.

- When Linda Blair vomited in *The Exorcist* (1973), the substance was made out of split pea soup and oatmeal.

- After Clark Gable opened his shirt to reveal a bare chest in *It Happened One Night* (1934), sales of undershirts fell nearly 40 percent.

- Cedric Gibbons (1893-1960) has the distinction of having had his name appear on the credits of more than 1500 films. His 1924 contract stated that every film released by MGM in the USA would give him the credit of Art Director, even though others did the majority of the work.

- In the film, *The Godfather* (1972), Marlon Brando, who often does not learn his lines for a film, had to have his lines written out for him and placed on various locations around the set.

- After being unemployed for many years following his starring role in the "Our Gang" series, Spanky McFarland placed the following ad in a Hollywood trade magazine: "Childhood (3-16) spent as leader of Our Gang comedies. Won' t someone give me the opportunity to make a living in the business I love and know so well? Have beanie, will travel."

- Shelly Winters performed her own swimming stunts in *The Poseidon Adventure*.

- W.C. Fields, jealous of co-star Baby LeRoy, once spiked the child's bottle with liquor. The shooting for the day had to be called off because of the child's drunkenness.

- Robert Redford has broken his nose at least five times.

- Tom Cruise may have looked good in uniform for *Top Gun* (1986), but in reality, he could never have become a naval pilot because the Navy requires that officers be 5 feet 10 inches tall, and Cruise is only 5 feet 9 inches tall.

- Cinderella is the story which has been remade the most— some 94 times! This includes cartoons, ballet, opera and parody versions.

- The animated dwarfs in *Snow White and the Seven Dwarfs* (1937) were modeled on real people.

- *Who Framed Roger Rabbit* contained 743 name credits (1989)—the most ever.

- Lillian Gish has the longest movie career of any actress, having debuted as a 19-year-old in *An Unseen Enemy* (1912), and making her last appearance in *Whales of August* (1987).

- When Walt Disney Productions released *Return to Oz* in 1985, it represented the longest time span that had ever occurred between the original and the remake of a film.

- At one time, the line "Let's get outta here" had been used in 84 percent of Hollywood movie productions.

17

TAXES
By J.C. Walker

Hysterical Markers

- Among the first recorded taxes in European history was "heregeld," a tax to pay for the armies of English monarchs who chose to fight the Vikings who were overrunning the countryside. Apparently, their efforts weren't hugely successful since most of what archaeologists know about the coins used to pay the tax were found in ruins in Scandinavia. An unpleasant side effect of these invasions still remains in the English language. The expression "to pay through the nose" came about from the 9th century Danish occupation of Ireland during which they couldn't exactly be called gracious guests—obstinate Irishmen who refused to pay the Danes' poll tax had their noses slit.

One For You, Nineteen For Me

- The Internal Revenue Service is trying hard to rectify its old image as Tax Man Tough Guy by spreading the word about its newest program—the Taxpayer Advocate. While representatives won't go to bat for you at an audit like an accountant, their job is to cut through bureaucratic red tape for problems, such as erroneous Social Security numbers or mislaid payments. The branch has about 450 staff positions around the country, including a field officer in each of the 33 IRS districts. In 1996, 300,000 cases passed over Advocate desks, which of course is a drop in the rather large bucket of 119 million individual tax returns. But every year branch officials also report to Congress on the problems that most often plague taxpayers in their dealings with the IRS. The biggest complaint? Tax code complexity.

I Wuz Robbed

- Many people don't realize that the IRS regards any and all income as taxable, whether gained by legitimate means or not. When infamous Chicago gangster Al Capone received a verdict of guilty in his trial for tax evasion on what he said were legitimate businesses, he exclaimed, "This is preposterous! You can't tax illegal money!"

Prove It

- The IRS estimates that of almost one million personal bankruptcies in 1996, 10 percent were fraudulent. That adds up to about $6 billion in revenue lost to the government, so the agency pays close attention to the details of taxpayers who can't or won't pay their bills—it files nearly 150,000 proofs of claim in response to that many bankruptcy filings.

This Town Ain't Big Enough For The Both Of Us

- The entire town of Morris, Alabama, recently had to face the music at tax time. Seems that the usual taxes were subtracted from employee paychecks, but actually paying the IRS that amount had been carelessly overlooked. Not amused, the agency called the Morris bookkeeping folks and stated that if they didn't get their check soon, the IRS would shut down the town. The language may have been a little strong, but in reality it meant that town employees wouldn't be paid, effectively ending services. City officials, needless to say, were stunned, although the town clerk had been dealing with the problem for more than a year as a "paperwork error." The $60,000 debt meant layoffs for three full-time and four part-time employees, including the clerk.

That's A Big 1040

- Actual real live tax forms and schedules we hope we'll never use:
  –Form 4563 Exclusion of Income for Bone-Fide
     Residents of American Samoa

–Form 1045 Application for Tentative Refund

–Form 6197 Gas Guzzler Tax

–Form 8328 Carry-Forward Election of Unused Private
  Activity Bond Volume Cap

–Schedule R Generation Skipping Transfer Tax

–Schedule P Credit for Foreign Death Taxes

–Form 4461-B Application of Master or Prototype
  Plan, or Regional Prototype Plan Mass Submitter
  Adopting Sponsor

–Form 5407 Application for Determination of Master
  or Prototype, Regional Prototype, or Volume-
  Submitter Plans

–Form 5213 Election to Postpone Determination as to
  Whether the Presumption That an Activity is
  Engaged in for Profit Applies

Inevitability

- It may seem incredible to taxpayers in the West, but China did not have a national tax system until 1994. As you might imagine, there are still a few kinks to work out, not the least of which is a hostile and uncooperative citizenry. Tax revolts are common throughout the enormous country, and matters of principle become life or death situations. A farmer in Shandong Province was told he was $57 in arrears to the tax commission, and he flatly refused to pay. A small army of officials arrived in his village to persuade him to cough up the money, and they found the man wired with explosives. Grabbing one official, he detonated the bomb, and the get-together was over. Like many others, a business manager in the city of Shenzhen named Gu Shaoguang found a loophole in the new tax system and filed false invoices to the tune of $12.8 million in tax rebates. The Chinese decided it was time to show the taxpaying population that it was "dead serious" about tax cheats, reports claim, and Gu was executed.

Holy Terror

- Wondering where your tax money goes isn't exactly a new phenomenon, either. During the Crusades, King Henry II of

England decided it would be a good idea to tax the citizenry heavily in order to sufficiently do God's work and to free the Holy Land of the tyranny of the Moslem invaders. Unfortunately, Henry got a little carried away with the whole idea and never bothered to actually redistribute most of the cash. Historians believe that the disastrous campaign against Saladin in the Holy Land failed because of an undernourished and underequipped army of Crusaders, and not because of their spiritual flaws as was claimed at the time.

Booked Up

- If you think you'd like to try preparing your own tax return, there are plenty of books available that can help. Even if they don't, at least a few of their titles might brighten your mood a little: *Taxes for Dummies*, *The Complete Idiot's Guide to Doing Your Income Taxes* and *Brilliant Deductions* are among the choices.

- Tires used for highway driving are subject to an excise tax if they weigh more than 40 pounds.

Illrgitimi Non Carborendum

- The English verb "to pay" is derived from the Latin word "pacare," which means to pacify, appease, or make peace with.

Pay Your Dues

- Taxpayers have a short, delusional French dictator to thank for their tax bill every year. During a 27-year period of the Napoleonic Wars, the English National Debt rose from 273 to 816 pounds, crippling the British economy. Prime Minister Pitt levied the first income tax to fight Napoleon's armies and to retire some of that debt. Even then, people complained about taxes—there was an outcry of protest when it was learned the tax rate across the board was a flat 10 percent.

Tax Byte

- In the mid-1980s the IRS put a lot of effort, time and money into its gargantuan computer system, and the big fella began having fits and starts only after a year or two. That system is a major contributor to the woes of the agency today, and if you look at the numbers, it's easy to understand why. The

IRS claimed that with the new system, it would be able to do a laser-screen preliminary audit on every single tax return filed, and subsequently set about doing so. The result was an average $4,770 tax bill for each taxpayer unfortunate enough to have a return that didn't match the "norm." All those bells and whistles still didn't guarantee total accuracy, and within a few years the IRS had to admit the electronic auditors were wrong 64 percent of the time. A later review by the General Accounting Office found that millions of taxpayers received computer-generated messages in 1987 in which the IRS claimed they had outstanding tax bills—the GAO determined 48 percent of these notices were also incorrect.

Tired Of It All

- "I owe the government $3,400 in taxes. So I sent them two hammers and a toilet seat." *– Michael McShane*

The More Things Change...

- We may think tax code books are huge and unwieldy, but so was one of the first records of taxation which was compiled in England by William the Conqueror in the 11th century. Ominously tabbed "The Domesday {Doomsday} Book," it was a record of who and what should be taxed, and is generally regarded as the instruction book for the tax collectors in the fulfillment of their job duties as well as a record of the results.

First American Tax Still Paying Its Way

- The first tax levied in America is still paying its way. The Constitution of the United States gave Congress the sole right to levy taxes. Congress first used its tax powers in 1789 when it levied a tariff on sugar. Tariffs were the chief source of federal revenue until the outbreak of the Civil War. Now:

The U.S. sweetener industry continues to pay a large share of deficit-reducing taxes, while pumping $26.2 billion into the economy and creating 420,000 jobs. U.S. sugar and sweetener farmers help to reduce the deficit by paying a special marketing tax. Under U.S. sugar policy, a special tax producers pay on every pound of sugar that's marketed raises more than $40 million per year for federal budget deficit reduction. The sugar program does not cost taxpayers anything. Our current U.S. sugar policy has not only helped reduce the federal budget deficit, but has resulted in low, stable sugar prices for American consumers. Our country's sugar farmers are highly efficient. Able to compete successfully with sugar and sweetener farmers around the world, U.S. farmers also provide higher wages, workers' compensation, environmentally sensitive controls, and other societal and federally mandated benefits. Since 1990, our sugar prices have declined. Americans pay 28 percent below what consumers in other developed countries pay, according to a study by a renowned international research firm.

- I filed my taxes electronically to speed things up, and it worked. I got an audit letter in half the normal time.

Taxation With Less Frustration

- Why tax your brain at tax time trying to remember where you put those important documents? Get organized! Getting organized at tax time can save you both time and money and might be easier than you think with these tips from the Sentry Group.

- Protect yourself from a paper avalanche. Set time aside weekly to divide papers into two piles—items needed for record keeping, items that hold interest for you and items you don't want or need. Throw the second pile out immediately.

- Create an appropriate fire-safe storage area for the papers you keep. Fire damages or destroys nearly 2,000 homes every day in the U.S. and can reduce newly organized records to ashes.

- Follow these guidelines on what to put in your fire-protective container and how long it should stay there:
  - Birth and death certificates–indefinitely.
  - Contracts–seven years after contracts expire.
  - Deeds–indefinitely.
  - Tax records–at least six years. Some tax forms must be kept longer.
  - Bank and credit card records–six years.
  - Health records–indefinitely.
  - Mortgage, loan papers–three years after the loan is paid off.
  - Insurance policies–four years from expiration date.
  - Home and property inventory–indefinitely (update as needed)
  - Marriage certificate, divorce, custody, adoption papers–indefinitely.
  - Passport–indefinitely.
  - Stock and bond certificates–four years after they're sold.
  - Owners manuals and warranties–as long as you own item.
  - Wills–indefinitely.
- If papers or belongings are valuable or irreplaceable, use an Underwriters Laboratories (UL) classified fire-resistant storage container.
- If important records, including tax information are kept on your computer, protect your computer files and make frequent backups. Store computer disks in specially engineered computer media storage containers, such as UL-classified Sentry Fire-Safe computer media chest or file.

18

PEOPLE OF FAME & FORTUNE

By Mona Lee McKown

An Unusual Millionaire

- When Hetty Green died in 1916, she was considered to be the richest woman in the world. She had a fortune of about $100 million. She was known as "the Witch of Wall Street" and was totally mad. She wore the same black dress for years and years, and eventually the dress turned green and then brown because of age. She used old newspapers collected from trash baskets as undergarments and lived on a diet of onions, eggs and dry oatmeal. Her unheated home was in the Chelsea section of Manhattan.

Hetty Green (the Witch of Wall Street)

A penny saved is... Wonderful

Hetty Green's fortune started from the $6 million she inherited from her father and grew through the accumulation of investments she made in the stock market.

A 97-Pound Weakling

- At the age of 11, Angelo Sicilian moved from Italy to Brooklyn. At that time he was a husky young boy, but after the move he became sickly and grew so weak that he could not climb the steps of the flat where he and his family lived. Angelo was a 97-pound weakling. He was so weak that one Halloween he was beaten by a boy with a sock full of ashes. When he was 16, while visiting the Brooklyn Museum, he noticed a statue of Hercules. He was so enthralled with Hercules' muscles and physique, he joined the YMCA a week later. He began lifting weights and exercising. It was then that skinny little Angelo became obsessed with strength. Through various exercises, he developed a chest that could expand to 54 3/4 inches and biceps of 17 inches. People at the gymnasium were so impressed they told him he looked just like the statue of Atlas on the bank building around the corner. "Atlas" became his nickname, and later he legally changed his name to Charles Atlas.

Queen Of Egypt

- Cleopatra VII was the daughter of Ptolemy XII. History is unclear which of Ptolemy's wives was Cleopatra's mother, as there were no records showing that information. She was born in 69 BC in Alexandria during the 300-year Macedonian dynasty of the Ptolemies in Egypt. Cleopatra was considered to be a descendant of the goddess Isis. Although she was not really take-your-breath-away beautiful, she was considered good-looking. Cleopatra did have strong appeal as she was sensual, sophisticated, witty and very intellectual. She began her rule of Egypt in 51 BC at the age of 17, and she married her brother, Ptolemy XIII, who was 10 years old. It was the custom of the time for sisters and brothers of the royal family to marry each other. She was able to rule for about two years before she was ousted from Egypt. After the battle of Alexandria in 47 BC, Julius Caesar, her lover, helped restore her position to the throne. During the battle, her husband was drowned, and she later married her younger brother, Ptolemy XIV. Julius Caesar remained Cleopatra's lover until his assassination in 44 BC. They had one child between them, Cesarion. Some two years later, Cleopatra became Mark Antony's mistress. They also had children, a set of twins and a younger son. Antony and Cleopatra remained together until 30 BC, when they both committed suicide.

Breaker Of The Bank

- Charles Wells was a very capable roulette player. In 1890, he broke the bank at the Monte Carlo roulette table a total of 15 times. Then in 1891, he returned to try his luck again. He was successful at breaking the bank five more times.

Who Gets The Dollars?

- Before America entered World War II, more than a million dollars was deposited in American banks. The money belonged to Adolf Hitler and other prominent Nazis. The money is still there today, and no one knows what to do with it.

What Is Wealthy?

- In 1776, if you made $4,000 a year, you were considered wealthy.
- In 1915, the average annual income for a family in the United States was $687 a year.

Money—It's Their Bread And Butter

- Cornelius Vanderbilt died on January 4, 1877, as the richest man in the United States. His estimated worth at that time was more than $100 million; $90 million went to his son, William Henry Vanderbilt, who increased his inheritance to $194 million by the time he died in 1885.

- Marcus Licinus Crassus lived in the Roman Empire from 115 BC to 53 BC. By the time of his death he had increased his inheritance of seven million sesterces to about 170 million sesterces. At that time this enormous sum was nearly equal to the annual income of the Roman treasury. He gained his wealth through many lucrative businesses. One instituted by Crassus was a 500-men fire brigade. In Rome there had not been a fire department prior to this. At the first warning of a fire, Crassus would send his men running, ready to fight the fire. Upon arriving they would stand and watch the flames, as Crassus bargained with the property owner over the price of the fire fighters' services. If a satisfactory price could not be obtained, Crassus would let the structure burn to the ground.

- In 1978, Daniel K. Ludwig was the richest man in the United States and perhaps the world. He was born in South Haven, Michigan, in June 1897. Ludwig quit school after the eighth grade. After the separation of his parents, he moved to Port

Arthur, Texas, with his father. While in Port Arthur, he sold supplies for sailing ships and steamers. He moved back to Michigan and worked at a marine-engine plant for 20 cents an hour. His work was so highly regarded by the plant management that they sent him on assignment to Alaska and the Pacific Northwest. At age 19, he quit the plant to go into business for himself. It was not until 1930, when he was 33 years of age, that he found a way to become one of the wealthiest men in the United States. His idea was to have oil companies charter unbuilt oil tankers from him for future delivery. After acquiring the charters, he would then use them as collateral to get the necessary loans to build the ships. By the mid-70s he became one of the world's largest independent ship builders. The size of Ludwig's fortune had not been confirmed, but educated guesses put it in the ball park of about $3 billion.

The Cherry Sisters

- The four Cherry Sisters were from Iowa. They left their home in 1893 to hit the stage and bright lights in Cedar Rapids. They performed a skit which they wrote themselves. They continued performing throughout the Midwest for the next three years. They performed to packed audiences, not because they were so good, but because they were so bad. The audience sometimes responded by throwing vegetables, so the Sisters always carried a portable iron screen which they could quickly erect on the stage and still continue their performance. Then in 1896, they received their really big break. They were offered the chance to perform on Broadway for $1,000 a week. In seven years' time, they had earned $200,000 and decided to retire from the stage.

A Miser of the 18th Century

- Daniel Dancer and his sister lived in England during the 18th century. The Dancers earned 3,000 pounds annually from their farmlands in Harrow, which is just south of London. Even with this annual income, Daniel was extremely stingy. He was often seen walking along the country roads, picking up cow dung and putting it in his pockets to take home for use as fertilizer. He would also hunt for old bones, using whatever meat was on them for their dinner and then giving the bone to his dog. The two Dancers sometimes received charity from people in the area. In one particular instance, a woman gave them a trout stewed in claret. It was a very cold evening, and when Daniel was bringing the dinner home, it froze. He did not want to eat the delicious meal frozen, and he did not want to waste any wood in trying to thaw it out over a fire, so he decided he would sit on the dinner, like an old mother hen, until it thawed.

Famed Words

- Before her last flight, Amelia Earhart left a letter to her husband stating, "Please know that I am quite aware of the hazards. I want to do it because I must do it. Women must try to do things as men have tried. When they fail, their failure must be but a challenge to others."

Quotes by the Rich and Famous

- "Wealth is the means, and people are the ends. All our material riches will avail us little if we do not use them to expand the opportunities of our people." – *John F. Kennedy*
- President Theodore Roosevelt died in 1919 and his last words were, "Please put out the lights."
- Farouk was the King of Egypt, and he died in Rome in 1965 where he was in exile. His final words were, "There will soon be only five Kings left: the Kings of England, Diamonds, Heart, Spades and Clubs."

Lover of Canines

- The Earl of Bridgewater was a Prince of the Holy Roman Empire. His name was Rev. Francis Henry Egerton. He lived the last few years of his life in the Hotel de Noailles in Paris. He was also a scholar and a patron of the arts. Each evening he would have an unusual formal dinner with 12 guests. The dinner itself was not unusual, but the guests were. The guest list was always made up of dogs. The dogs always sat in armchairs with napkins tied around their necks, and each had a servant standing nearby to attend to their every need. After the meal was over, the canine guests would accompany the Earl in his carriage for a spin around Paris.

Work of Artist is Famous

- Warner E. Sallman was born in Chicago in 1897. His parents were both European-born and attended the Evangelical Covenant Church. Sallman went to the Art Institute of Chicago and began his career as an illustrator for religious publishers and advertising agencies. He had been assigned to come up with a suitable illustration for the *Covenant Companion*, a magazine. He had a deadline to meet the next day, but was not able to draw a single line on his paper. Finally, he went to bed, giving up for the night. At 2:30 in the morning, he woke up and recalled later, "Suddenly, there appeared to my mind's eye a picture of the Christ just as if it were on my drawing board." The next morning Sallman hurriedly sketched the picture he saw in his mind and got it to the magazine just before the deadline. Sallman's picture is one known to millions throughout the Christian world. The image of Jesus has flowing hair, blue eyes, a well-barbered beard and mustache and a warm transcendental look. More than 500 million copies of "Head of Christ" have been printed since 1940.

Everyone Has His Price

- Many gamblers called Arnold Rothstein "The Big Bankroll" because of his idiosyncrasy for never going anywhere unless he had $100,000 in cash in his wallet. He was also known to take huge risks when he gambled. At one time he bet $250,000 on the turn of a card.
- One-fourth of the world's population lives on less than $200 a year, and there are 90 million people who survive on less than $75 a year.
- In 1978, the average American family had to earn at least $17,106 a year to be considered "living moderately well."
- In the United States, there are more female than male millionaires. Females comprise 50.4 percent of the total.

19

FASCINATING "FIRSTS"

by Kathy Wolfe

First Things

- The first bifocals were worn by Benjamin Franklin, who also invented them as the solution to his eyesight problems. He was nearsighted and had trouble reading, so he had two pairs of glasses. He grew tired of continually changing back and forth between the two pairs, so he had the top half of the distance glasses cemented to the bottom half of his reading glasses.

- A young freshman at Harvard University originated goldfish swallowing in 1939, and it soon became a craze.

Harvard education develops a sense of taste

- Nylon stockings first went on the market in 1939, manufactured by the DuPont Corporation.

- The first fully electric kitchen was exhibited at the 1893 World's Fair in Chicago. The first motor-powered dishwasher was put on the market in 1911.

- Doctors first used X-rays to reveal broken bones in 1895.

- The word *restaurant* comes from French, meaning "restorative," with the first public eating establishment open for business under that name in 1765. Thirty-some years later, there were more than 500 restaurants in Paris alone.

- The first modern golf ball was developed by B.F. Goodrich.
- Kitty litter first hit the market in 1947. Its ingredients are ground clay and baking soda.
- Nine dollars was paid for the country's first television commercial—an ad for the Bulova watch in 1941.
- New Haven, Connecticut, was the home of the nation's first phone book.
- On baseball's Opening Day, it is tradition for the president to throw out the first pitch. This started in 1910 when President William Howard Taft began this custom.
- Doctors were first able to listen to patients' hearts with a stethoscope in 1925.

First Folks

- Why are Elliot and Ruth Handler famous? They created the first Barbie doll in 1959, naming her after their only daughter.
- The first person to go over Niagara Falls was Anna Taylor in 1901. She did so in a cushioned barrel. Adding to Anna's daring was the fact that she could not swim.
- The first U.S. president to be born in a hospital was Jimmy Carter.
- Abraham Lincoln, elected in 1861, became the first president to wear a beard.
- The first policewoman hired was in 1910 in Los Angeles.
- Franklin D. Roosevelt was the president who appointed the first woman to a cabinet position, Frances Perkins as Secretary of Labor. FDR was also the first president to appear on television.
- In 1891, Whitcomb Judson was the first to come up with a novel idea for the textile industry—the zipper.
- The first African-American to be signed on by the NBA was Nat "Sweetwater" Clifton, who began playing for the New York Knicks in 1950. This occurred four years after the birth of the NBA.
- It was department store entrepreneur Marshall Fields who first said, "The customer is always right," in the 1880s. It was the department store's concept of fixed prices that put

an end to the bargaining and "haggling" over prices previously used in the marketplace. It was also when prices ending in $.99 first appeared, as competition heated up.

- Hyman Lipman earned $100,000 for his clever invention in 1858—the first eraser on the tip of a pencil.
- Albert Berry made his claim to fame when he became the first man to parachute from an airplane. Albert jumped from an altitude of 1,500 feet on this momentous day in March of 1912.
- Gertrude Ederle was only 19 when in 1927 she became the first woman to swim across the English Channel, with a time of 14 hours, 31 minutes.
- Ranchers might not recognize the name of Joseph Glidden, but they are forever in his debt. Glidden received the first patent for barbed wire fencing in 1874.
- Although the name Louisa Swain is not a famous one, she draws fame for being the first woman to vote legally, back in 1870. Although voting was not legal in the United States, it was in Wyoming Territory where Mrs. Swain lived.
- Silas Noble and James Cooley were granted a patent in 1872 for the world's first toothpick manufacturing machine.

More Firsts

- It was from a Civil War hot-air balloon that the first aerial photograph was taken.
- The term "reality check" was placed in the dictionary for the first time in 1997 editions. This popular term is defined as "a proof or test of the truth of a belief or opinion by comparison with known fact."
- If you had visited Jacob's Pharmacy in Atlanta, Georgia, in May of 1886, you could have been the first person ever to taste Coca-Cola. At the time of its introduction, only about 13 glasses a day were being sold. It wasn't called "Coke" until three years later. And three years after that, physicians were questioning whether Coca-Cola caused cocaine addiction.
- Although Coke became a bigger seller, Dr. Pepper debuted before it. Dr. P. was acclaimed as a "tonic, brain food, and

exhilarant," and went on sale in Waco, Texas, in 1885. After an over-protective father terminated his daughter's engagement, the jilted young man named the new drink after his almost-father-in-law.

- The Labor Day holiday came along in 1882, designed to be a holiday for the working class; it was celebrated with a parade of 30,000 marchers in New York City.
- It was in 1908 in Superior, Montana, that Bibles were first placed in hotel rooms by the group known as the Gideons.
- The Polaroid camera developed and printed snapshots right in the camera beginning in 1948.
- It was the state of New York that initiated the use of the electric chair for execution in 1890. It was hailed as "a humane alternative to hanging."
- 1931 was the year Americans first tasted Twinkies, Bisquick, Toll House cookies, and Alka-Seltzer.
- It was not until 1880 that an American woman received a Ph.D. And it was not from an American college, because no American schools offered that degree to women students. Martha Carey studied overseas, and was awarded her degree at age 23.
- Acclaimed as "perfect for Americans on the move," self-serve cafeterias made their debut in Chicago in 1893.
- The Diamond Match Company introduced a cardboard folder with 20 paper matches and a striker pad in 1896—the first book of matches.
- We started squirting cheese out of an aerosol can in 1966.

Up in Space

- The "race to space" began in October of 1957 when the Soviet Union launched the first artificial satellite into space. *Sputnik I* traveled at a velocity of more than 17,750 mph.
- While the United States was the first to put a man on the moon, we were not the first to launch a manned spacecraft. The U.S.S.R. was ahead of America by about three weeks with this achievement in April of 1961. The next month, Alan Shepard was the first American to go up into space. Yet, he

was not the first to orbit the earth. That honor belongs to John Glenn, the following February.

- The U.S.S.R. was also the first country to put a woman in space in 1963. The United States didn't catch up with this one for 20 years when Sally Ride went up in the space shuttle *Challenger* in 1983.
- It was not until 1930 that the planet Pluto was first seen. The sighting was made from an observatory in Flagstaff, Arizona.

Introductions

- Children in America attended kindergarten for the first time in 1856 in Watertown, Wisconsin.
- In 1914, Marcella Gruelle came across an old doll of her grandmother's, and had her cartoonist father draw up a design from it. The result was the first Raggedy Ann doll.
- Folks began saving S & H Green Stamps in 1891 when Thomas Sperry came up with this novel idea.
- 1935's Chicagoland Music Festival introduced a new event, the first of its kind ... the baton-twirling contest. This spurred interest, resulting in the publication of *The Complete Book of Baton Twirling* as well as regularly updated versions of *Who's Who in Baton Twirling*.
- How long have you been putting Cool Whip on your desserts? Since 1965, when this nondairy item made with sorbitan monostearate and xanthum gum was introduced.
- There were no cantaloupes in America before 1818. That's when seeds were brought to Germantown, Pennsylvania, from the country of Tripoli.
- Americans first stopped at a drive-in bank in 1946 in Chicago. Tellers behind heavy bullet-proof glass slid drawers out to motorists for their transactions.

Never Before

- The "pneumatic carpet renovator" came along in 1899. Today we call it the vacuum cleaner.
- Prior to 1828, circus performers wore short jackets and knee pants with stockings. One evening, the time of bareback rider Nelson Hower's performance neared, and his costume still

had not arrived. He was forced to do his act in his long knit underwear. They were so comfortable and versatile, it wasn't long before most of his co-workers were wearing tights.

- Sardines have been sold in those little cans for a long time— since 1876. Back then, the cans consisted of three pieces soldered together, and were first marketed in Maine.
- Four out of five Americans use vendors' cents-off coupons. The first coupon was a "penny-off," issued by the Post Cereal Company in 1895.
- Phi Beta Kappa became the first fraternity in America in 1776 at William and Mary College in Washington, D.C. Today it has about 425,000 members nationwide.
- It was in 1932 that the words "Snap! Crackle! Pop!" first appeared on the Rice Krispies box. However, the little characters bearing those names did not come along until a year or two later.

Post Office News

- Thomas Brown has the honor of inventing the mail box in 1810. He went on to become governor of Florida.
- We've been licking postage stamps since 1842, when they could be bought for 3 cents.
- It took the first Pony Express rider in 1860 59 minutes to travel 20 miles. The cost of mailing a letter by Pony Express was $5.00 per half ounce.
- Letter carriers began wearing uniforms in 1868.
- The first woman's photo to appear on a postage stamp was Queen Isabella's, the one who financed Christopher Columbus' 1492 journey. Martha Washington's was the first American woman's.

Interesting Firsts

- Camden, New Jersey was the site of the first drive-in movie theater, grand opening date June 6, 1933.
- Business must have been slow in the undertaking profession in 1891, at least for embalmer Almon Strowger. He took time out of his schedule to invent the first dial telephone.
- The first president to be married in the White House was

Grover Cleveland, who, at age 49, married his 25-year-old ward, of whom he had been guardian since she was orphaned at age 14.

- Two German fellows obtained a patent in 1852 for the first electric whale-killing machine.
- The Frisbie fad began in 1957 and the Hula-Hoop mania a year later. Before the "Hula-Hoop" name stuck, it was marketed as "Whoop De Do" and "Hoop Zing."
- Folks began reading Batman comic books in 1939.
- The 1904 St. Louis World's Fair was the site of the introduction of iced tea. The English gentleman operating a tea booth on this very hot day was dismayed at his lack of business and came up with the idea to boost sales.
- Motorists crossed the Golden Gate Bridge in San Francisco for the first time in May of 1937. This grand opening followed nearly four and a half years of construction, during which 11 workers were killed.
- America's first orphanage became necessary in 1654 when a boatload of orphaned children from Holland was sent to New York City.

20

COFFEE
by J.C. Walker

- "Coffee should be black as hell, strong as death, and sweet as love."   — *Turkish Proverb*

Just Call It Java

- Coffee is an ever-present fact of our everyday lives, yet it is a complicated foodstuff that contains an "alphabet soup" of chemical components most of us have never heard of. We all know about the purine alkaloid known as caffeine, but coffee also contains liverine, paraxanthine, theacrine, and theophylline. Among the carbohydrates in coffee are arabinose, fructose, galactose, glucose, and sucrose; but it may come as a surprise that it also contains calcium, magnesium, phosphate and potassium.

Sibling Rivalry

- There are numerous species of coffee throughout the world, but only two are what we would think of as "coffee." "Coffea Arabica" and "Coffea Canephora" are their Latin names, and traders and roasters call them arabica and robusta beans. Arabica is the aristocrat of the two, and it is primarily used for gourmet coffee and cappucino. Robusta has a less delicate aroma and flavor, and its purpose in life is as processed and instant coffee. Needless to say, the robusta bean is tougher and more disease resistant, and it can stand lower altitudes with hotter growing conditions. In addition to being sturdier, it also packs a bigger caffeine whollop than its Arabica sibling, which makes it useful as a filler, too.

To Bean Or Not To Bean

- Coffee was originally used by the Galla tribe of Ethiopia about 1000 during long treks across the desert. They'd grind it and mix it with animal fat for a quick blast of energy on the trail. Its use quickly spread to Yemen, where the beans actually originated, and then on to Arabia where monks cultivated it in their oasis gardens. Although it was still used for food and sometimes medicine, it wasn't long before they used the grinds in boiling water to create a popular drink they called "qahweh," which, roughly translated, means "prevents sleep."

Just Another Bean Story

- There's a myth about one of these monks who is credited with the discovery of the effects of coffee. He was strolling down a mountain trail one day when he spotted a goat herd dancing and leaping about the hills, joined in a sprightly fashion by his herd. Apparently, the young man, whose name was Kaldi, found that even his old and tired goats would perk up after eating the bright red berries from nearby bushes. Kaldi shared a few of beans with the weary traveler who was amazed by their rejuvenating effect. He hurried home to share his discovery with his brothers, and evening services took on a fervor not seen for many years. Although this story was written by an Arab author named Rhaziq in the early 800s and is considered fictional, it is the first account of coffee in any literature in the world.

Doesn't Get Any Better Than This

- Just when you think "gourmet" can't get any weirder, this just in: The trendy new taste for people who home brew is mocha beer. The recipe contains hops and yeast, of course, but also four ounces of Ghiradelli chocolate and two cups of brewed coffee.

- "Ah! How sweet coffee tastes! Lovelier than a thousand kisses, sweeter far than muscatel wine! I must have my coffee!"
  – Johann Sebastian Bach

Do Me A Flavor

- We don't think much about the words "Blended Coffee" on the label, but this is the way coffee merchants get the vast array of flavors with the exotic names and enticing aromas. Each coffee growing region produces beans with distinct personalities due to their unique growing conditions, and these differences are what make it possible to offer blends with exotic names like Macadamia Nut and French Vanilla. Every country has a reputation for certain flavors and qualities in its coffee. For example, the Dominican Republic is said to have beans that are "strong and heavy bodied with a mild acidity factor," Ethiopia has beans with a "winey and fruity taste with a mild acidity," while Guatemalan coffee has a "rich, spicy, or smoky flavor."

- Africa is the place where coffee got its start and where it is cultivated to a large degree today.

- A neutron goes into a coffeehouse and asks the waiter, "How much for a cappucino?" The waiter replies, "For you, no charge."

Throw Out that Ginseng

- Status-conscious China recently opened its doors to massive coffee consumption, and of course, gourmet coffee wasn't far behind. A well-known Seattle gourmet coffee company has opened six coffeehouses and stores in trendy, Western-style shopping centers, and there are plans for additional shops in Shanghai, Hong Kong, and Guangzhou.

Sedimental Journey

- Coffee was embraced by almost every society it touched around the world, and not surprisingly, its irresistible lure invited controversy and intrigue wherever it went.

- In 1453 coffee was introduced to Constantinople by Ottoman Turks, and the first coffee shop opened there in 1475. Turkish law still makes it legal for a woman to divorce her husband if he fails to provide her with a daily quota of coffee.

- In 1511, the governor of Mecca, Khair Beg, banned coffee as he feared its use would encourage political opposition to his dominion. The Sultan replied to his worried message with sentiments that coffee was sacred, and then ordered the governor executed.

- In 1600, advisors to Pope Clement VIII recommended he ban coffee as a conspiracy of the "infidel threat." His response was to "baptize" coffee and render it an acceptable Christian drink.
- In 1700, Charles II of England banned coffeehouses as "hotbeds of revolution." Unfortunately, it was too little too late for Charles: The ban lasted 11 days.
- In 1732, Johann Sebastian Bach wrote Kaffee-Kantate, which at first glance is an ode to coffee. In reality it was a political protest to the movement seeking to ban coffee drinking by women.
- In 1773, the Boston Tea Party demonstrated the American colonies' unwillingness to be taxed by King George III for items considered necessities. The ultimate result was that the rebels turned to coffee as the everyday drink of choice and never went back to drinking tea.

Coffee to Curl Your Toes

- Recipe for authentic American Cowboy Coffee: Place a kettle of cold mountain water over your campfire. Throw ground coffee in the pot and bring to a boil. Take it off the fire and crush the shell from one egg and throw it in the pot. Now settle back, and enjoy the sunrise; wait for the aroma to rustle up the crew. We have to warn ya: It ain't halter broke.

– The Cowboy Coffee Company

You'll be a Better Person for Knowing This

- Ever wonder why coffee leaves those distinctively recognizable rings on every surface it touches? A physics professor at the University of Chicago challenged his colleagues to hash out the complicated problem, and this is what they learned: Spilled coffee spreads quickly on the counter and comes to a halt when thinned and stopped by the invisible abrasion of the countertop. The coffee is now "stuck" within its own limits, and can't shrink or grow.

Evaporation begins with the edges constantly replenished with liquid from the interior of the stain. It carries the few small solid particles in the liquid which build up around the edges and result eventually in a dried ring.

Leaded and Loving It

- A six-ounce cup of brewed coffee contains 100 mg. of caffeine, slightly more than twice the amount in a equal-sized portion of tea, and more than three times as much as a caffeinated cold tablet.

Airport Disaster

- Here's a true coffeeshop horror story from Ottawa. A woman has a few minutes at the airport before her husband's plane arrives, so she decides to kill time with a cup of coffee and a candy bar at the concourse coffeeshop. Magazine, Kit Kat bar, and coffee in tow, she pulls up a seat at a small table and begins to read. Suddenly, the man sitting next to her picks up the Kit Kat, opens it, and breaks off a piece. Incredulous, the woman defiantly breaks the second piece and pops it into her mouth. He breaks off the third piece and gobbles it up. Enraged, the woman grabs the fourth piece and glares at the man as she eats it. The man orders a chocolate donut, at which point the woman grabs it and stuffs as much as possible in her mouth. The man, visibly angry, stands up, tosses a few coins on the counter and storms off. Confused by the whole episode, the woman finishes her coffee and then rises to leave. She opens her bag to pay for the coffee and discovers a pristine, untouched Kit Kat bar in her purse.

Choose Your Poison

- While we take caffeine for granted as one of the benefits (or disadvantages) of coffee drinking, in reality the coffee plant evolved loaded from top to bottom with it as a powerful natural defense. With no thorns or spines to protect itself, the plant instead packs a huge dose of caffeine in its most vulnerable parts—new leaves, buds and seeds—to repel insects, bacteria and fungi. Not only will this kill most plant predators, but the caffeine washed off the plant and on to surrounding soil also discourages the growth of other plants who would compete for available water, nutrients and sunlight. Ironically, it is also caffeine that makes coffee so irresistible to humans, resulting in its cultivation all over the world and assuring its survival.

Coffeehouse B.S. (Before Starbucks)

- Coffeehouses have a history almost as long as coffee drinking, and one wonders if the stimulating effect of the beverage is the reason that these were places of intellectual exchange and often radical activism. Historians believe they got their start in Persia around 950, and even then, they were places where gentry and thinkers would meet and share political or philosophical views. The buildings were sumptuous palaces open from early morning to late at night, and it was common for scholars, poets, officials, and well-to-do locals to visit on a daily basis. Unfortunately, coffeehouses in Persia gradually became less intellectual and more notorious as time passed, so that eventually those visits were not considered a proper activity for "respectable" men.

- The first coffeehouse in Italy opened in 1645, and the first in England in 1652. Again, especially in England, they became the places where educated men could meet and exchange ideas. In time they were the principal social centers in major cities, and learned and uneducated people alike gathered together to debate current affairs. The charge for coffee was a penny a cup, and, given the nature of intellectual exchange, coffeehouses became known as "penny universities." They also are the source of a pervasive custom we observe today— "to insure promptness" patrons would give the server a small coin, now referred to as a TIP.

Bean There Done That

- Long before coffee beans arrive at your neighborhood coffeehouse, they have traveled on an arduous journey and faced much potential abuse during picking, washing and roasting. Coffee beans start as bright red berries that ripen at varying rates, so part of the expense of the more flavorful coffee is the requirement that they be hand-picked individually at the peak of ripeness. Then they are washed, and the seed (what we think of as the bean) inside is removed, either by a machine or by sun-drying and hulling. Roasting is the most critical variable. Some gourmets insist it must be done on a very small scale and strictly by instinct, and others maintain that highly technical machine roasting renders the best results. One tool of the scientific types is a machine to classify the darkness of roasted beans, called the Agtron. Using near-infrared light to measure the carmelization of the bean sugars, the scale runs, in a complete absence of logic, from 25 (the darkest) to 95 (the lightest).

- Ethiopia produces some of the most valued beans in the industry. It began with an advantage few other countries had —flourishing coffee plants growing and thriving in the wild. Probably for that reason, Ethiopian coffee is characterized as "wild and spicy."

Unleaded

- Coffee beans are decaffeinated in one of two ways. In the first, unroasted beans are steamed and then saturated with a solvent for about half a day. Another solvent is applied to remove the first solvent, and the beans are rinsed with steam for another 10 to 12 hours and then dried. In the second or "indirect" decaffeinating method, the beans are almost boiled for just a few hours, which does a fine job of removing the caffeine, but also takes out most of the things that make coffee taste so good. The remaining liquid goes through a process where just the caffeine is removed, and the beans are boiled in it again to restore the flavor.

- Don't think that all that caffeine then passes into the great Compost Beyond. It is sold to pharmaceutical and soft drink companies to add zip to their products!

- The famous Swiss beverage company Nestle has added another decaffeinating method to the list. It recently closed a deal with an Australian biotechnology company to perfect their methods of growing genetically altered coffee plants that produce beans with no caffeine at all.

Out of Africa

- In Kenya, officials worry that erratic El Nino weather patterns do more than ruin a few vacation days—the upset of rain patterns significantly affects production of a major cash crop. A nonexistent rainy season in the spring gets things off to a bad start, and then torrential rains in the usually dry fall completely set the Kenyan coffee industry on its ear.

- In Uganda the major obstacle to a successful coffee industry isn't the weather, but politics. Those who remember the '70s will also remember the dictator Idi Amin's unpleasantness of that time, and during that era, coffee production fell from an average of four million bags per year to two million. In 1997, well over four million bags were again produced.

Kona Krazy

- Although more coffee is consumed in the U.S. than in any other country in the world, very little coffee is produced here. The only significant amount is grown on the southwestern slopes of the Big Island of Hawaii near the town of Kona, hence the name "Kona Coffee." Because of the limited suitable real estate for coffee growing, only about 20,000 bags a year are produced, and coffee addicts gladly pay the higher prices for the beans considered a delicacy by those in the know. Beans are grown on the volcanic slopes of Mauna Loa and Hualalai, in what are considered to be exquisitely ideal conditions of high altitudes, warm, sunny mornings, and moist, cloudy afternoons. There is no historical record of frost ever having been there, and the island's isolation has protected the crops from disease and insects. The coffee has been characterized as "rich, with a velvety body, and mild, delicate aroma."

- Big Islanders are justifiably proud of their coffee production, and every year in the fall they celebrate with the Annual Kona Coffee Festival, the oldest food festival in the state. Coffee lovers can revel in more than 30 coffee-related events, among which are the Kona coffee picking contest, Kona coffee farm and mill tours, Kona coffee cupping competition, Kona coffee art exhibit, Kona coffee recipe contests and the Miss Kona Coffee Scholarship Pageant.

Buzz Off

- Scientists in Massachusetts completed a ground-breaking study, so to speak, about the actual effects and counter-effects of coffee and booze on the human body. In their book entitled *Buzz: The Science and Lore of Alcohol and Caffeine*, they confirm and refute a number of myths we've all accepted about what these substances actually do to our bodies. For example, they contend women are more sensitive to alcohol not because they are smaller, but because the alcohol-destroying enzymes, their stomach linings don't work as efficiently. The scientists offer proof that coffee can help offset the effect of too much alcohol in the system. They also say that alcohol doesn't "kill" brain cells, but it does affect every functional system in the body because it is so powerful a drug.

The Final Fact

- We may joke about caffeine addiction, but it's for real. Coffee withdrawal lasts about five days and is characterized by blinding headaches, irritability, lethargy, nervousness, and mild depression.
- "After the coffee things ain't so bad." – *Henry Herbert Knibbs*

Coffee Blues

21

NASCAR AUTO RACING
By J. C. Walker

The Sport

- There are dragster races, midget cars, the modified series, Indy cars, the USAC National, and the Silver Crown, but the king of all race car competitions is best known as NASCAR—the National Association for Stock Car Auto Racing. Now boasting the highest spectator numbers in the world, the sport began humbly after World War II when young men were returning to Appalachia with new mechanical expertise and a hunger for excitement. Many of them had family histories of supplementing incomes by distilling and delivering home-made beverages on which they preferred not to pay taxes, so the requirement for responsive, fast cars quickly became a business necessity on the winding mountain roads of the Carolinas and other Southern states. It was only natural that these lean and mean vehicles would soon become a popular form of recreation in that part of the world, and stock car racing was born.

- The first stock car race was held in 1949 in Langley, Virginia. Incredibly, several drivers rented cars in order to compete. While many drivers are still based in North Carolina, generally considered the "home" of the sport, their teams now haul themselves, vehicles and equipment to 32 races at 19 tracks around the country. They're shooting for the championship of all these races (by earning the highest number in cumulative scores) rather than victories in individual races that may be more or less demanding depending on the track.

- Spectators may fantasize about racing for the Winston Cup in the family Monte Carlo or Grand Am, but in reality the cars that compete in NASCAR bear no resemblance to their namesakes once you look under the hood—there's really not much that's from "stock" there. Their 450-horsepower engines can propel the cars to 200 miles an hour, and the vehicles average a cost of no less than $150,000 each.

Stock Shock

- Stock car drivers such as Dale Earnhardt, Mark Martin, Bill Elliott, Jeff Gordon, Rusty Wallace and Dale Jarrett are among the "big winners" in NASCAR, and their salaries and careers can take on rock-star proportions. More realistically, many of the less-well-known drivers earn about $30,000 in salaries, and their staff positions are filled by volunteers. Making it big can create big headaches.

- A crash in Charlotte several years ago completely totalled the car, but the junked parts were still worth $97,000.

- Really successful drivers operate their teams on budgets in the neighborhood of $5 million, with most of their costs going not for parts on the vehicles but for labor to keep them going. Research and development as well as transportation and housing costs on the road are huge expenses. Owners often maintain more than a dozen cars in order to race at different tracks with different requirements.

- And NASCAR is definitely a part of the '90s scene—a few teams have several airplanes and as many as half a dozen public relations staff people.

Smokin'

- When NASCAR drivers say a race is really hot, they aren't kidding. Heat from the engine and the exhaust systems in the race cars can top temperatures of 1600 degrees Fahrenheit, so it's no surprise that shields on the cars are now made of the same material that protects space shuttles from the sun in space. While we may picture space-age technology and white-coated scientists scurrying around testing heat levels, in reality the thermal protection systems were developed because the Kennedy Space Center director is a NASCAR fan. When talking to drivers, he'd learned that cockpit temperatures often reach 160 degrees, and drivers have had their feet blistered two inches deep from holding down the pedals. The problem has grown even worse in recent years because the cars are increasingly aerodynamic and air flow has been continually minimized. While that may help the vehicle move faster, it means the chance to cool off drivers is also diminished. Rusty Wallace's team took his car to the Kennedy Space Center where it was outfitted with thermal blankets of spun ceramic and glass protection, installed under the seat. Testing revealed that the cockpit temperature was reduced by 50 degrees— bringing it to an almost balmy 110 degrees.

Jenny Craig Need Not Apply

- Never let it be said those great guys at the NASCAR home office aren't fair—they recently decided that drivers who weigh under 200 pounds will have additional weight added to their vehicles in order to eliminate their advantage over heavier competitors.

Boys and Their Toys

- It's not so uncommon now to hear of grown men attending baseball camp, space camp, football camp—and now you can fulfill your auto-racing fantasy literally in the fast lane. It helps if you have time to spare and money to burn. Set high above the glittering lights of the Las Vegas strip, the Autopian Motorsports Country Club awaits the realization of your dreams. Membership includes perks not even thought about until a few years ago: access to single-seat Formula cars, Ferrari 348s and exotic sedans, professional auto racing lessons, modification of owners' own cars, attendance at high-profile NASCAR and Indy car races, introductions to celebrity drivers, souvenir equipment and clothing, and members' names stenciled on their cars next to sponsor logos. Under construction is a $4-million clubhouse that will overlook the 1.5-mile tri-oval Las Vegas Motor Speedway and will feature a 7,000-square-foot garage facility in its basement. Memberships in this new kind of country club will cost between $20,000 and $25,000 a year.

What Could Go Wrong?

- Tim Allen of TV's "Home Improvement" fame thought he'd participate in a lark in the Daytona International Speedway GTS-2 division of the Rolex 24-hour sports car endurance race last winter on driver Steve Saleen's team. "Steve told me the most I would have to do was three hours, and I thought, 'I could do that.' He didn't tell me he meant 'at a stretch.' I thought I would drive three hours ...and then watch these guys do all the work. Then Steve informs me, 'That's three hours, the other guys do three hours, then you get back in after a little nap.'" Tim thought long and hard before living up to his commitment: "The last endurance race I drove was from my home in Detroit to Colorado to see my grandmother, in a Ryder truck."

Fast Fact

- Officials estimate that 31% of NASCAR fans are women.

No Gender Gap

- Fans of Indy car racing already know that women have been participating in the Indianapolis 500 races for more than 20 years. Janet Guthrie broke the gender barrier in 1976, and several other women have followed in her footsteps. When Guthrie arrived there, it had been only a few years since prohibitions against women's entering the pits and the garages had been lifted, and there were no garage restrooms for women. Although she received substantial media attention for simply being the first woman driver there, she received little public applause for her accomplishments. While she couldn't qualify that first year, Guthrie did so the next at 188.403 mph. In 1978 she qualified 15th, drove 190 laps and finished ninth—with a broken right wrist that forced her to shift left-handed across her body.

- Lyn St. James, who was named "Rookie of the Year" at that race in 1992 and has competed every year since, also admits she gets a lot of media focus because of her gender. While much of her time and attention goes toward preparation for Indianapolis, she is also getting attention for the driving school she has started—a school designed primarily to develop young women with a burning desire to become race car drivers. More than 62 students have taken her course at the Indianapolis Raceway Park during the fall, and she has discovered drivers with strong potential that range in age from 8 years to college age. This project is part of St. James' overall plan to become a team owner.

- Women are race car drivers, race car fans, and now they are making money in race car competition, too. One of the most successful wholesale merchandising companies marketing NASCAR-sanctioned products has a CEO named Lidia Lewis. "Racing USA" had sales of $12 million in 1997, and the company sells products with a NASCAR theme that range from bumper stickers to area rugs to high-end leather jackets, as well as apparel, like tank tops, biking shorts, and bathing suits. All the items feature faces or signatures of the likes of Dale Earnhardt, Jeff Gordon and other top drivers. Lewis believes the loyalty demonstrated by auto racing fans is a big part of her success—marketing experts have found that 70 percent of racing fans report they "almost always" choose NASCAR sponsors' products over similarly-priced brands, as opposed to 31 percent of basketball fans, 36 percent of football fans, and 16 percent of Olympics '96 viewers.

22

FOOD FACTS

by Kathy Wolfe

- "To the man with an empty stomach, food is God."

  – Mohandas Gandhi

First Fact

- The term *hors d'oeuvres* literally means "apart from the main work"—that is, before the main course.

From Fruit to Nuts

- The word *fruit* comes from the Latin word *frui*, which means "enjoy."
- About 80 percent of the world's grape crop is used in the making of wine. Only 13 percent is consumed as fresh table grapes, with the remainder used for raisins, juice and jellies.
- If bananas ripen to yellow on the tree, they will lack taste or will rot. This is because their starch turns to sugar, and the skins break open. For this reason, bananas are picked green and are allowed to ripen during shipment.
- The mechanical cherry picker did away with the need for manual labor. This machine shakes the cherry tree until the fruit falls onto cloths under the tree.

- Apples are 85 percent water.
- If someone asks you for a Northern Spy, a Rhode Island Greening, a Gravenstein, or a Winesap, they're checking

whether you have an apple. There are more than 7,000 different varieties of apples.

- Linguine, the pasta, translates from the Italian word meaning "tongues."
- The blue veins in bleu cheese are actually mold.
- If you're munching on arachides, goobers, mani, or pinders, you are eating peanuts. The country of India produces more peanuts than any other in the world. Peanuts develop underground, 1 to 3 inches down, and when ready to harvest, are dug up and flipped over to dry in the sun.
- It seems strange that Grape Nuts are called by that name. They have neither grapes nor nuts in them. When Charles Post invented them, he originally called them Elijah's Manna.

Vegetarian Fare

- If you ask for hushpuppies down South, it's not a pair of shoes you're after, but fried cornmeal fritters. They received their name at outdoor fish fries when they were fed to barking dogs to keep them quiet. While the dogs yapped, the cook yelled, "Hush, Puppies!"
- Don't be deceived into thinking that margarine has less fat than butter. Both are 100 percent fat. And they both have the same number of calories.
- One cucumber plant can yield up to 100 fruits.
- The next time you eat corn on the cob, count the number of rows. It will almost always be 12, 14 or 16. It is rare for an ear of corn to have an odd number of rows. On an 8-inch ear of corn, there are between 600 and 700 kernels of corn.
- Some famous vegetarians were Shakespeare, Leonardo da Vinci, Benjamin Franklin, Charles Darwin, and Albert Einstein.

You Say Potato–I Say Potahtoe

- We eat more potatoes than any other vegetables. And we eat more of those in French fry form than in any other style.
- While vacationing in Saratoga Springs, New York, in 1853, Cornelius Vanderbilt ordered French fries. But when they arrived at his table, they were too thick for his liking. He

sent them back to the chef. The chef, George Crumb, was miffed by this act, and to show his irritation, he shaved the potatoes paper-thin and fried them. They were an instant hit. What started out as an act of revenge led to one of the nation's largest businesses—the potato chip.

- Vichyssoise is a leek and potato soup. It is served cold and topped with chives. It receives its name from the Vichy region in France, a valley rich in potatoes.

Where's the Beef?

- The population of the U.S. consumes more than a billion hot dogs each year. The French, on the other hand, are fond of frogs, devouring more than two million of those hoppers every year.
- Before you order chitlins off the menu, you may want to know they are the small intestines of pigs.
- Dark turkey meat contains more fat and calories than white meat.
- Some folks in Great Britain are fond of eating hedgehogs. They first encase them in clay, then bake them. When the clay is peeled off, the spines and skins come off. The taste of a hedgehog is similar to that of pork.

Junk Food Junkies

- Dentists conducted an experiment, giving one group of children a can of pop every day for three years and the other group water. The kids drinking pop had 50 percent to 150 percent more tooth decay than those drinking water.
- Oreo cookies have been around since 1912, when they were introduced as the Oreo Biscuit and could be purchased for 30¢ a lb.
- The world's best selling cookie is the Oreo. But it can't top the largest cookie ever made, which measured 35 feet x 28 feet 7 inches and contained more than 3 million chocolate chips.
- Tootsie Rolls were named after creator Leo Hershfield's girlfriend, Tootsie.
- When you're drinking root beer, some of the ingredients you're sipping are oil of wintergreen, vanilla, nutmeg and anise.

- Cereals ranking close to 50 percent sugar are Cocoa Pebbles, Honeycomb, Froot Loops, and Trix. Those low in sugar, 3 percent or less, are Wheat Chex, Puffed Rice, and Shredded Wheat.
- Popsicles were introduced in 1924. During the Depression, they were changed to Twin Pops so that two children could share one Popsicle.
- At the carnival years ago, if you asked for "Fairy Fluff," you would receive cotton candy.
- European monks brought pretzels into the world. Students who learned their prayers were given a pretzel as a reward. The crossed ends of the dough represented praying hands.
- The man who invented Graham crackers, Dr. Sylvester Graham, refused to indulge in the consumption of meat, tea, coffee, and tobacco, and opposed corsets and featherbeds.
- Looking for a cure for stale marshmallows? Place them in a sealed plastic bag along with a piece of fresh bread for three days. You will have soft marshmallows and stale bread.
- Forrest Mars and Bruce Murrie are responsible for naming their creation, M&Ms.
- Although popcorn seems to fill up the box of Cracker Jacks, it's not the principal ingredient—sugar and corn syrup are. This tasty snack made its debut at the 1893 Chicago World's Fair. But the box did not contain a toy prize until 1912.
- Except for supplying energy, sugar has no nutritional value.

I Scream, You Scream

- In 1930, baker James Dewar was dismayed that the strawberry season was so short, thus limiting his sales of shortcakes. In order to prolong his sales past the fresh fruit season, he experimented with filling his sponge cakes with cream. He called them "Twinkle Toes Shoes," but the name was later shortened to "Twinkies."
- Visit your local 31-flavor ice cream parlor and ask for a double-scoop. With 31 flavors, there are 496 different combinations you could receive.

- It's interesting that folks in Alaska eat more ice cream than folks in any other state in the Union.
- The five most popular ice cream flavors in the U.S., in order, are vanilla, chocolate, butter pecan, strawberry, and neapolitan.

Quick Sandwich Facts

- A group of folks from Hamburg, Germany, emigrated to the U.S. in the late 1800s, bringing with them a new and unique way of serving meat—in ground form. And so the "hamburg" (hamburger) was born. It was originally a meat pattie served between two slices of toast and was called a "Hamburg Steak."
- The first hamburger stand chain was White Castle in 1921. McDonald's didn't come along until 1940 when the McDonald brothers, Richard and Maurice, opened their own drive-in. In the 1950s, a milk-shake machine salesman out of Chicago, Ray Kroc, offered to go into the drive-in business with them. The brothers declined. Kroc bought them out, and began the McDonald's franchise in 1955.
- Depending on where you live, you'll order a long oblong sandwich at the deli by one of the following names, submarine, hero, hoagie, grinder, or wedge.
- The largest hamburger ever made weighed 5,520 pounds and was 21 feet across.

What's Up, Doc?

- Studies have shown that carrots seem to slow the progression of cancer. Pancreatic and lung cancers especially seem to be decreased with the intake of carrots. They are also beneficial in cutting down cholesterol, as well as in keeping the colon healthy. About two medium-sized carrots every day seems to be all it takes.
- In 1991, a gentleman in Great Britain grew a carrot 6 feet, 10.5 inches long. Another fellow in Great Britain kicked the cigarette habit by eating carrots. He ate up to five bunches a day and became very irritable when his carrots were withdrawn.

Good For You

- Garlic has long been considered therapeutic to your health.

For hundreds of years, it has been used in poultices, as an anticoagulant and an antiseptic, and in the treatment of dysentery, laryngitis, asthma, athlete's foot, bronchitis, and leprosy, just to mention a few.

- There is evidence that garlic could be a cancer preventative. A survey conducted on residents of a certain county in China where they eat seven cloves of garlic a day shows a remarkably low rate of cancer. The survey does not comment on their breath! They should know that chewing parsley is the most recommended remedy for "garlic breath."
- As far back as 3,000 years ago, boiled rice solutions were prescribed for diarrhea. Eating rice bran is also said to prevent kidney stones.
- Shellfish are believed to stimulate mental energy because of their large content of a certain amino acid, which, when released, energizes brain chemicals which cause us to be more attentive and motivated.

Quick Bits

- You would need nine quarts of milk to make one pound of butter.
- Rice is the main food for half the world's population.
- You've heard the expression "packed tighter than sardines." The oil that they are packed in is more expensive than the sardines, so it is more lucrative to pack more fish into the can.
- Do you know the difference between a frankfurter and a weiner? A frankfurter has a hog casing; the weiner has a sheep casing.
- If you're a steak lover, consider the fact that grasshoppers are about three times more nutritious than steak is.

Burn Baby, Burn!

- Since there are 3,500 calories in a pound of body fat, it makes sense that if you burn up 3,500 extra calories of energy, you use up that body fat. If you plan to spend an hour playing checkers, you'll burn about 80 calories; if you ride your bike during that hour, expect to use around 300 calories.

The Earl of Sandwich

- During the 1700s, The Earl of Sandwich, an English nobleman, was in the midst of a card game and didn't want to be interrupted. So, he ordered his servant to bring him two slices of bread with roast meat between them. His creation was named after him.

Chicken Little

- Harlan Sanders did not start up his Kentucky Fried Chicken franchise until age 65, after he had reached retirement. His first Social Security check helped launch his business. He sold out his interest in the company in 1964 for a reported $2 million dollars.

Plant-Caused Illnesses and Death

- In Ohio, a little girl was playing house. She picked some pretty red berries from a shrub growing in the garden and arranged them on a toy dish. She ate the berries, pretending they were part of her play-house dinner. She became sick a few hours later. Doctors figured out too late that she had eaten berries from the poisonous daphne plant.

- In Washington, a toddler died suddenly. He was rushed to the hospital where doctors believed he had choked on a piece of candy. After further examination, they determined that he had eaten berries from the nightshade bush.

Final Bits

- Did you know that most pancake syrups sold in the U.S. are actually only about two percent real maple syrup? The remainder is corn syrup and artificial maple flavoring.

- You can prolong the life of milk by adding two teaspoons of baking soda per quart. This will give it an extra day or two.

- Get your can opener ready—the average American household devours the contents of 788 cans of food each year.

- Your taste buds distinguish four basic tastes: sweet, sour, bitter, and salty.

- Louis Lassen opened the first hamburger stand in 1900 in New Haven, Connecticut. Seating capacity—three.

23

MOVIES
By J.C. Walker

The First Fact

- Hollywood heart-throb Robert Redford has been lighting up the screen for 30 years, and his presence onscreen still attracts moviegoers in droves, but he has received only one Oscar Award during his career—his role as director of *Ordinary People*.

Ten'SHUN

- The popularity of military films never seems to abate, and they present a variety of challenges unique in movie making. One of the biggest obstacles in movies such as these is that it's pretty difficult to rent, say, a battleship for a few weeks, so the Pentagon assists movie makers by allowing crews to use military facilities and equipment at cost. Naturally, the military prefers to see films depicting men and women in uniform as exemplary types, so Hollywood military critics don't always get the cooperation they would like if their portrayal is less than flattering. Films the military smiled upon: *Clear and Present Danger*, *The Hunt for Red October*, *Patriot Games*, *Renaissance Man*, and *Flight of the Intruder*. Some other films you've seen lately with a military theme were made without Pentagon approval and assistance.

Pentagon goes to the movies

OK the Butler doesn't do it..., It's a guy from the Coast Guard

...and the warm sensitive Marine is out.

SCRIPT

No Shades of Gray

- Carl Snavely's name isn't exactly a household word, but this football coach at Cornell University in the 1930s is responsible for much of the action of television and movie sports today. He was the first to realize there was value in reviewing home movies of his team's most recent games in order to see what his players were doing right or wrong. The flickering black and white films in his den in Ithaca, New York, changed other things, too—he was responsible for getting teams to wear white jerseys in order to make the opponents distinguishable from each other on the playing field.

Movie Madness, Big and Small

- In spite of home video, cable TV, and every other conceivable form of entertainment now available to the public, people still like going to the movies. Although attendance is down at first-run shows, there is still strong evidence that a night at the cinema is the fun people think of first.

- Last fall in Moscow, Kodak Company opened Cinema World, or "Kinomir" in Russian. Billed as a "one of a kind, state of the art" theater of 42,000 square feet, the complex features first-run Western films and a retail complex. There patrons can have their pictures taken and digitally super-imposed with any number of movie-star images, or they can purchase Hollywood apparel and merchandise. The theater itself seats 4,000, has a 40-foot-wide screen and a 38-speaker digital surround-sound system.

- Meanwhile, in Rushville, Illinois, the cinematic entrepreneurial spirit also lives. When the townspeople learned their last remaining theater in this small town of 3,300 was about to close, they had to take action fast. Since the town is more than an hour's drive from Springfield, opportunities for local recreational activities were disappearing, taking with them inducements for business and new residents to settle there. About 220 local citizens bought shares in the dilapidated Princess theater at $100 apiece, using the money for a sound system, marquee, projection equipment and furnace. Local kids and seniors tend the ticket counter, and sponsors estimate there may actually be dividends within a year or two. The only disappointment so far was opening night when the film *Apollo 13* broke, and the audience was left wondering if the astronauts made it safely back to Earth.

- Did you hear that Woody Allen is making his first nature film? It's the epic story of a neurotic salmon who wants only to float downstream.

That Tingling Sensation

- We might laugh about what used to be considered "special effects" in early films, but in the '50s, those effects could be very personal indeed—one of the promotional gimmicks of *The Tingler* was the installation of a vibrating buzzer in every theater seat. It was activated at particularly scary moments during the film.

It's Magic

- One of Tinseltown's best-kept secrets is that a star on the famous Hollywood Walk of Fame features a well-known public figure who was not an actor. Harry Houdini is honored with a star prominently placed in front of the venerated Chinese Theater, site of many opening-night shows over the years.

85 Percent of Success is Showing Up

- National attendance was down 15 percent at first-run movies in 1996 compared to 1995. There were 17.5 percent more movies competing in the marketplace, while at the same time production and marketing costs were at an all-time high. Movie executives claimed that a movie had to gross $10 million its first weekend of showing, or it would likely be a huge box office disaster.

Don't Blink

- Ten musicians who achieved their 15 minutes of fame as actors: The Yardbirds—*Blow Up*, 1966 as out-of-control rock band. Tom Petty—*FM,* 1978 as himself being interviewed.

Robert Cray—*Animal House*, 1978 as member of Otis Day and the Knights.

Patti LaBelle—*A Soldier's Story,1984* as no-nonsense barmaid.

Paul Shaffer—*This Is Spinal Tap,* 1984 as incompetent promotions guy, Artie Fufkin, of Polymer Records.

Lindsey Buckingham—*The Freshman,* 1990 as guitarist backing up Bert Parks.

Chris Isaak—*The Silence of the Lambs,* 1991 as SWAT team member storming library in search of Hannibal Lechter.

Kelly Willis—*Bob Roberts,* 1992 as the politician's duet partner, Clarissa Flan.

Eddie Vedder—*Singles,* 1992 as drummer for Matt Dillon's grunge band.

Julian Lennon—*Leaving Las Vegas*, 1995 as bartender interceding in mindless, alcohol-induced frenzy of Nicolas Cage.

Smokin'!

- Even though Americans have quit smoking cigarettes in record numbers over the last 20 years, this phenomenon would not be evident from movie characters depicted during that time. In a random sampling of scenes from 62 top-grossing films released from 1960 to 1990, overall tobacco use in the the movies remained the same. Even though smoking by the lead characters dropped a little, the numbers were still three times that of smokers in corresponding age groups in real life.

- People just aren't going to see movies in theaters like they used to, and it's really worrying the folks in the industry. Just the other day, I called to find out the movie schedule at the theater down the street. I asked, "What time does the feature go on?" The manager replied, "What time would you like it to go on?"

Go Boom

- Physicians are becoming worried that movie-goers are actually believing it's possible to emerge unscathed from the gruesome calamity of accidents, fire-balls, and explosions evident in movies today. In reality, the booms and crashes are getting more and more spectacular because they're usually computer-generated, putting the actors at little or no risk. The next time you see a movie hero crawling out of a smoking, twisted mass of wreckage that moments before was his convertible, remember in real life, doctors claim, he would look more like Jabba the Hut after eating pizza than James Bond after a night on the town.

King Tut's Curse—The Sequel

- One of the most prolific cinematic producers in the world is Egypt, which for many years was the only country in the Middle East to have a movie industry. Its film tradition goes back as far as that of Europe or the United States, as the first Egyptian movie was made by the French filmmaking pioneers, the Lumiere brothers, only a month after their first cinematic project was shot in France in 1896. Although much of the content and settings of the films are not familiar to Western moviegoers, a leading man in many of them is—Omar Sharif.

Santo Preserve Us

- One of the great unsung heroes of "moviedom" was a Mexican superhero in the early '60s known as Santo. This name was changed to Samson when the movies were imported north of the border, but Santo never changed his look or his approach to evil during his heyday of crime and monster fighting. Originally a well-known wrestler before entering the film world, Santo wore a dark skin-tight jumpsuit and mask throughout every movie, even when he was out for a spin in his snazzy convertible. The baddies he confronted were especially sinister—some Santo film classics are *The Robot vs. The Aztec Mummy*, *Sequel to the Aztec Mummy*, *Santo Against the Zombies*, *Santo Against the Vampire Women*, and our particular favorite, *Santo Against the Diabolical Brain.*

They Don't Make 'Em Like They Used To

- The World Wide Web Bad Movie Home Page choices for

the 10 worst movies ever made:

1. *Robot Monster* 1953
2. *Valley of the Dolls* 1967
3. *Glen or Glenda?* 1953
4. *Peyton Place* 1957
5. *The Brainiac or El Barron del Terror* 1961
6. *Plan 9 From Outer Space* (this selection is usually referred to throughout the industry as Probably the Worst Movie Ever Made) 1959
7. *The Creeping Terror* 1964
8. *The Tingler* 1959
9. *The Magnificent Obsession* 1954
10. *Airport* 1970

Or Look at Your Tax Return

• We may think that action figure dolls and fast-food campaigns are the ultimate in cinematic marketing promotion, but they pale next to some of the horror movie promotions of the '50s. The gimmick of the movie *Macabre*, for example, was truly inspired—ads offered $1000 life insurance policies if a movie-goer died of fright.

Steamed

• Many movie sets have been used so often they're almost as recognizable as the stars themselves, but not many also are distinguished as state historic parks. Railway 1897 is such a site in Jamestown, California, and it's been the locale for films such as *The Red Glove* (1919), *My Little Chickadee* (1940), and *Back to the Future III* (1990). Part of the California State Railroad Museum in Sacramento, Railway 1897 is as rustic and realistic as an old railyard can be. The site has been valued over the years not only for the outstanding collection of old buildings, engines and cars, but also for nearby terrain that varies from "Kansas plains" to "Arizona low desert" to "California gold mine." The site's biggest celebrity is Sierra No. 3, a 105-year-old steam locomotive which has had starring roles in 70 movies and television shows.

Names Not Up in Lights

- Even though actors and actresses don't change their names as willingly as they used to, there are still plenty who do. Some of the names that didn't turn heads are:

  Martin Sheen—Ramon Estevez

  Jane Seymour—Joyce Frankenberg

  Susan Sarandon—Susan Tomaling

  Susan St. James—Susie Jane Miller

  Iggy Pop—James Jewel Osterburg

  Mike Nichols—Michael Igor Peschkowsky

The Last Look

- *Batman Forever* broke records for both highest opening-day box office gross and highest single-day gross by bringing in $20 million on June 16, 1995.

- "Movies are really realistic these days, but I think they're running out of ideas. I was walking down the street and saw a movie marquee that just said: *Dyslexia: Movie The*."

  – Tommy Sledge

- "Tomorrow is the most important thing in life. Comes into us at midnight very clean. It's perfect when it arrives and it puts itself in our hands. It hopes we learned something from yesterday."

  – John Wayne

24

"WHY WE SAY IT"
by Kathy Wolfe

The First Fact

- Why do we say, "That's a lot of bunk," meaning "That's a bunch of nonsense"? It's because of a North Carolina congressman, whose district included Buncombe County. This politician droned on and on for hours in a speech that was largely unrelated to any issues at hand, refusing to relinquish the chair even when called upon to do so, claiming he was "making a speech for Buncombe," which turned into a lot of bunk.

A Point From The Pen

- Does the term "What the Dickens?" have anything to do with author Charles Dickens? Actually, not a thing. It's just another way of saying "What the devil?" and was used by William Shakespeare in *The Merry Wives of Windsor* long before Charles Dickens was even thought of.

The Jewelry Nook

- The brachium is the medical term for the forearm. Ancient Greek soldiers who engaged in hand-to-hand combat were often injured on their forearms, so devised a protective band for that area. Their word for this heavy piece of leather was "bracel," and precious metals were often used to decorate these bands. Whenever a woman wore some sort of jewelry around her wrist, it was referred to as a bracel-et, or "little bracel."

- Mr. Forney was an early maker of cheap jewelry whose business was to create brass rings to resemble gold as closely as possible. They were hawked by street vendors for a much more reasonable price than the real thing. It wasn't too long before the articulation of the word began to change, and "Forney rings" graduated to "Phony rings," then broadened out to mean anything that wasn't genuine.

• Playing your trump card often wins the card game, which means you "triumph" over your opponent. "Trump" is merely a condensed version of the word *triumph*.

"That's The Way The Money Goes"

• If someone hands you a "C note," you've been given $100. We call it that because the Roman numeral for 100 is "C." Now if you're in possession of a "G note," you have a $1,000 bill, not because "G" is the Roman numeral for 1,000, but because "G" is short for "grand," the slang expression for $1,000.

• The word *tip*, referring to the gratuity left for a restaurant server, dates back to 17th-century England, when patrons at taverns and coffeehouses dropped into a box on the wall a coin which was given to the waiters. The purpose of the money was clearly stated on a sign nailed on the box—"To Insure Promptness," which was later shortened to just the initials of the three words, T.I.P. The German interpretation of

Why do we say TIP

HUMBUG!

To Insure Promptness

$

"tip" is *Trinkgeld*, or "drink money," and was given by the customer to a waiter to buy himself a drink.

• The old Anglo-Saxon word *sceot* referred to "money put into a general fund," the same as our taxes today. In early times, this tax was based on the person's capacity to pay.

• Early Italian money-lenders operated from behind a bench or counter called a *banca*. When, for whatever reason, the

Italian went out of business, his place of operation was totally destroyed with the *banca* broken apart. The Italian word for "broken" is *rotta*, so when the counter was demolished, it was *banca rotta*, which is why we call someone who is financially insolvent "bankrupt."

- Animal lovers may object to the song "Pop Goes the Weasel," fearing for the welfare of the poor weasel. However, the word *weasel* originally was the slang term for purse or pocketbook. And isn't it true, "That's the way the money goes?"

The "Heinz 57" Of Sayings

- Why is the Pope called the Pope? It's simply because the Italian word for "father" is *Papa*, modified into "Pope."
- The old English word *fortnight* means a time period of two weeks and is merely a contraction of 14 nights. Likewise, *good-bye* came from "God Be With Ye."
- "Let's mosey on down the road" is a popular American expression. But it takes its roots from the Spanish word *vamose*, which translates "Let's go." The same Spanish word is the source for "vamoose," so "Let's go leisurely" and "Let's go in a very big hurry" have the same ancestor.
- We began calling criminals "thugs" because the Hindustani word *thag* translates to "cheat" or "swindler"

On The Job

- In days gone by, the privilege of having carpet in an office was reserved for the boss alone. Whenever an employee was called into the boss's office, he stood on the carpet, leading us to our term "called on the carpet," for being chewed out or scolded.
- You're sure you've got the job; matter of fact, it's "in the bag," a term borrowed from the world of hunting. Some prey might get away, but not the one that's been shot and put in the bag.
- "Here's the man for the job" was shortened to "That's the boy," which was further condensed to "Atta boy."
- You've spent days working on a new presentation. The day arrives when you meet with the boss, only to have him

exclaim, "Someone else showed this to me last week!" Someone has "stolen your thunder." This phrase originates from what happened to a virtually unknown 17th-century dramatist, John Dennis, who, although pretty much a failure at writing plays, did manage to invent a machine that simulated thunder for use onstage. After one of his own ill-fated plays closed at an English theater, he found his thunder machine was being used without his permission in the production of *Macbeth* at the same theater. He shouted in fury, "See how the rascals use me! They will not let my play run, and yet they steal my thunder!"

G.I. Joe

- Anything distributed to the army by the U.S. Government was referred to as "Government Issue," or "G.I." for short. The term progressed to refer to the soldiers as well.

- Around the time of World War I, the British were conducting experiments involving airships for warfare. Two designs were introduced and tested—the "A-limp" and the "B-limp," called such because they were limp, non-rigid dirigibles. The "A-limp" proved to be a failure; however, the "B-limp" was successful, and the name was modified to the word *blimp*.

Bull's Eye!

- At the center of every target is the bulls-eye, a red circle. In early times in France, this center was white. Since the French word for "white" is *blanc,* and their word for "aim" is *point*, we received our term "point-blank," which refers to being aimed straight at the mark with the target very close.

Monkey Wrenches In The Works

- A monkey-wrench has nothing to do with monkeys. This wrench, which can be adjusted to fit different sizes of nuts and has a movable jaw, was invented by a blacksmith named Charles Moncke.

Bobby–Soxers

- As women in the 1920s "bobbed" or cut short their hair, during the 1950s socks were "bobbed," or made much shorter, hence the term "bobby socks."

No Bones About It!

- You're having guests for dinner. You've prepared a delicious fish chowder, but you've inadvertently missed removing one of the fish bones during the preparation. Fortunately, the guest who receives the bowl containing the bone is very polite, and discreetly disposes of it, without making any mention of the bone. Somewhere along the course of time, the phrase "making no bones about it" changed from a gesture of politeness to a boldness of speech.

"Chew The Fat"

- Without refrigeration, the mainstay of early sailors' diet was saltpork, which would not spoil because of the method of its preservation. All parts of an animal were used when preparing supplies for a voyage, and a sailor was frequently fed a tough bit of skin with a layer of fat on it. As sailors sat on deck griping about their provisions, their actions became known as "chewing the fat."

The Real McCoy

- An obnoxious drunk was pestering a famous prizefighter named McCoy, egging him on to fight. But McCoy knew his own strength and abilities, and, after assessing the man's condition, he adamantly refused to fight. The drunk's cronies attempted to dissuade him, informing him that this man was McCoy, the prize fighter, but to no avail. The drunk continued his harassment, and McCoy finally hauled off and punched him, knocking him out. Once revived, the drunk proclaimed, "You're right! He's the real McCoy!" giving us our well-known phrase.

More "Why We Say This"

- Before we cook poultry, we clean the insides out. All of its guts are "plucked" out of its body. That's why someone who is brave or "has a lot of guts" is referred to as "plucky."
- To protect their thumbs from the prick of the needle pushing through fabric, early seamstresses placed a bell-shaped cap on their thumb. The "thumb-bell" became "thimble."

PJs

- The word *pajama* came to us in the 1870s from India when British troops brought back a new style of nightclothes. Translated from the Hindi language, it means "leg clothes."

You Don't Say...

- In the times of King Louis XV, French ladies retired to their private sitting rooms to pout. From the French word for "sulk," we derive the word boudoir, the name now given to the room.

- In the days after Indian reservations were established, it was illegal to sell liquor to Indians. However, those greedy for cash found a way to sneak the liquor onto the reservation— stuffed into the top of their tall boots, giving us the word bootlegger, which refers to one who sells liquor unlawfully.

Quick Bits

- In the days of slave trading, ship captains were perpetually concerned about slaves' breaking free of their bonds and causing a murderous riot. As an extra precaution, the guards slept on deck rather than in the hold to be near the prisoners. They built small shelters to sleep in, which were so uncomfortable they became known as "doghouses," which went on to represent other undesirable places to be in.

- Perhaps you received a bit of news that made you "tickled to death." This originates from an old method of punishment in China where victims were actually tickled to death as their torture.

- In Norse mythology, Odin, the god of storms, happens to be attended to by a dog, who represents mighty gusts of wind. The myth portrays a cat as heavy rain. Combine the two, and you have a storm where it "rains cats and dogs."

Very Interesting Stuff

- Conjoined twins are those who are joined somewhere on the body, often the hip, chest, or head. They occur approximately once every 50,000 births, and are always of the same gender. The first set to become widely known were Chang and Eng, who were joined at the ribcage. These famous twins were born in Siam (which is now Thailand) in 1811, giving us the term "Siamese twins." They married sisters and between them fathered 11 children and lived to the age of 63.

- Early Romans held the belief that those people who were insane were "moonstruck." As the moon advanced toward the full stage, derangement supposedly worsened. Since the Latin word for "moon" is *Luna*, our word "lunatic" evolved.
- Combine chicken broth, milk, diced chicken, and mushrooms and serve on toast, and you have chicken ala king, supposedly named for King Edward VII of England, to whom this concoction is attributed.
- The Dutch word for "trumpet," *bazu*, lends its meaning to two American words "bazooka," a rocket launcher with a bell-shaped end, and the vibrating musical instrument "kazoo."
- It's thought that the word *bacon* comes from the German word *Bachen*, or "wild pigs."
- A certain Scottish weaver of the early 1800s sold a large order of wool fabric to a store in London. On the invoice, the London business was billed for the yardage of "tweel," which is the Scottish variant of "twill." The Englishman misinterpreted the term, calling it "tweed," and our name for rough woolen cloth was born.

The Last Look

- "He's just trying to get a rise out of you" is a term derived from fishing. Have the bait at precisely the right spot, and the fish will rise to it and be caught.
- "We should have a great many fewer disputes in the world if words were taken for what they are, the signs of our ideas only, and not for these things themselves." *– John Locke*
- "A word is not a crystal, transparent and unchanged; it is the skin of a living thought and may vary greatly in color and content according to the circumstances and time it was used."

– Oliver Wendell Holmes Jr.

25

GARBAGE
By J.C. Walker

Take This Job and Recycle It

- Americans may believe that they do a lot of recycling at home, but the workplace is a far more environmentally correct place than the typical household. In 1992, the commercial percentage of disposed trash was 43 percent while 57 percent came from residences. The office is into recycling—in the same year 27 percent of recyclables came from offices and other workplaces while only 17 percent came from homes. These numbers are changing, though. It's estimated that by the year 2000 the residential percentage of trash will go down to 54 percent and that the recycling rate will go up to 27 percent. The commercial recycling rate, on the other hand, will also rise to 32 percent.

Designer Hell

- Seattle is now far more than the site of famous coffee houses and scenic views. It has a new claim to fame as the birthplace of designer compost. A compost company there recently released its new product line as one that is entirely plant-based, smoother, better-smelling and more plant-enriching. At $20 a cubic yard, this compost is said to be far superior to the competitor's. A gardening expert was quoted as saying that it looks pretty much like any other compost no matter how you shovel it.

- And if compost is now designer, can garbage cans be far behind? Soon a new line of colored trash bags will be available to match a well-known brand of garbage cans, all sized appropriately, of course. The company has not announced the specific colors as yet, nor has it stated if mix and match options will be available.

Out of the Closet

- There is hope for the chronically junk-disadvantaged. "Professional organizing" is a rapidly growing field, and they are ...well-organized. They have their own association called the National Organization of Professional Organizers, and most members believe that being organized is a genetic gift and that some people just have an "organizing gene," encouraging them to lead lives of tidiness. The rest of us, however, will pay an organizer $25 to $50 an hour to clean our closets, straighten the garage, and muck out the kid's rooms.

Dumped On

- Non-New Yorkers think of Staten Island as the picturesque destination of the famous Staten Island Ferry and as a small and still-rural borough of New York City. Less well-known is that for 50 years Staten Islanders have complained about their home being the repository of New York City's garbage. More than 14,000 tons of refuse a day has been hauled and dumped there, and the landfill now occupies 10 percent of the Island's dry land. Residents claim the pile of garbage now towers higher than the nearby Statue of Liberty, more than 151 feet.

And I Thought the Remote Was Under the Sofa Cushion

- A day at the beach is, uh, not exactly a day at the beach any more. Trash and debris left behind by those seeking sand and surf are reaching epidemic proportion, and federal officials are trying to draw attention to the fact that the culprits are not off-shore vessels. A recent cleanup of American beaches by the Center for Marine Conservation found evidence that it's everyday folks who regard the beach as a handy spot to unload that bothersome garbage. In a one-day sweep that covered 43 states and U.S. territories, the following items were found:

- 800,358 cigarette butts
- 24,407 disposable cigarette lighters
- 135,613 aluminum cans
- 8,081 car tires
- 28,611 plastic foam fast food containers
- 27 television sets
- one remote control
- three VCRs
- 20 mattresses
- 14 refrigerators

It's a Living

- The world's most-appreciated garbage man is Gabe Tovarez, a long-time resident of Tucson, Arizona. On his 1,000-stop garbage route throughout a nearby retirement community, Gabe takes the time to chat with his customers and gets to know them one by one. The residents respond to his friendliness with more than just waves and an occasional glass of cool water. He receives Christmas checks, invitations to anniversary parties and memorials, and recently someone named a dog after him. Not long ago, Gabe received the Driver of the Year Award from the Environmental Industry Association.

The Pits

- Five amateur archeologists have found a whole new niche, as it were, in history. They scour Brooklyn Heights neighborhoods in New York and ask residents who are remodeling if they can excavate the sites of the former outhouses behind the rowhouses there. In 1850 folks installed indoor plumbing as soon as it was available, and the outhouses were torn down, but people continued to use the pits as handy landfill dumps for household junk and debris. The historians have uncovered a variety of antique goodies from the late 1800s—the usual bottles and chamber pots, of course, but also ink bottles, false teeth, high-button shoes, unopened anchovy cans, soup bones, handpainted marble, toys and dolls, tools, books and magazines, and even cans of money.

What, No Biographies?

- Trash collecting and recycling at the summer Olympic Games in Atlanta gave new meaning to the phrase "Higher, Faster, Stronger." It's estimated 9,000 tons of trash were generated during the events, and visitors used color-coded containers for paper, cardboard, plastic and aluminum to recycle. Every night 150 trucks picked up and emptied 26,000 trash bins, and recyclers turned in more than 3,000 tons of paper and cardboard. Plans to mark the recycled paper with the official Olympic logo, however, have been scrapped.

A Breath of Fresh Air

- Scientists at NASA are searching for the remaining places on Earth without garbage. They're flying about the South Pacific with special air-sniffing machines, flying from island to island and looking for the cleanest air in the world. While it sounds like a project most of us would like to try as a vacation, the scientists are serious about what they're doing. They've discovered that the moisture and strong sunlight of the tropical oceans break down the ozone, hydrocarbons and pollutants produced by cars, smokestacks and (believe it or not) trees, and they want to learn more about this region of the world they believe is the world's biggest air purifier. The investigators do not expect to find a pollution-free area, however. In 1991 they found air pollution, which had originated in Europe, in the western Pacific.

Clean Sweep

- The city of Madras in India has never been known as a tantalizing destination for world travelers. If anything, the city was noteworthy for its particular lack of interest in collecting and clearing garbage off the street. Citizens finally had enough, however, and several neighborhoods embarked on a program known as Exnora—an acronym for "excellent, novel, and radical." What's novel and radical is that households are each paying 10 rupees a month to neighborhood "street beautifiers" who spend a few hours a day collecting garbage from each apartment and taking the assortment by bicycle to the city landfill. This excellent improvement in city living has resulted in individuals planting trees and sweeping the streets in front of their homes.

Where No Garbage Truck Has Gone Before

- What really sets us apart from animals is the human ability to litter, no matter where we are. Of grave concern to NASA officials in Houston is the growing amount of junk that's been left out in space for future astronauts to clean up. Old rocket bodies, lens caps, bolts, paint chips and rocket fragments are only some of the odds and ends now circling the globe, and scientists estimate that much of the junk will continue to do so for millions of years since the items will not deteriorate. While some of it will flame out as it falls into the Earth's atmosphere, most of it will not, and the problem is that even a paint chip one millimeter in diameter, traveling at 10 kilometers per second, can easily tear holes in a space suit. Large junk, such as burned-out weather satellites, pose a real threat in future high-atmosphere exploration. NASA refers to them as "fossil-projectiles."

You Can Take It With You

- Bonnie Gilpin of Grand Island, Nebraska, is well known about town for her inability to throw anything away. In fact, she cruises sidewalks and alleys for additional stuff to add to her collection, which rises to the ceilings of her small home. She gathers broken baby strollers and empty beer cartons and various other debris scooped up ahead of the garbage hauler. Gilpin was jailed in the late '80s for piling trash as much as 4 feet high in her front yard, so apparently moving her collection indoors was an attempt to accommodate the city fathers. In fact, she accumulated so much stuff that both front and back doors are blocked, so she climbs up a ladder and crawls in an open window when she wants to get inside. Court hearings are pending.

Perfect for Pocket or Purse

- After the deadly poison gas attack in subways by a radical cult group, Tokyo officials yanked out every trash receptacle in every station to foil any other potential saboteurs. While Americans might assume this move would instantly result in a huge, overnight trash heap, the results in Japan were remarkable. The Tokyo subway stations are cleaner than they were before the incident throughout the entire 147-mile system. Transit officials report staff are spending less time cleaning stations than at any other point in history. The Japanese simply will not throw their litter on the pavement (it's considered poor form to make a mess), and as a result, commuters carry wads of paper and tissue in pockets and handbags throughout the work day. Sales of newspapers are down 20 percent in station kiosks, and beverage companies have complained to the government that their business has been seriously affected as well.

Demolition Derby

- We may feel like we're doing our part to recycle when we pitch that pop can in the right bin, but what do you do when you're a demolition company, and you're faced with discarding items like steel beams, punched-out drywall, old lumber and pieces of concrete? Companies have found landfill fees to be prohibitive for this kind of waste, and environmentalists are concerned at the space requirements. Companies are developing methods, however, which will render this kind of junk manageable and perhaps even usable. Crushers, shakers, screens, and magnets are all used to separate the jumble of junk produced by demolition crews, and leftover wood can be used in power plants for composts and mulch and in making paper. Even gypsum drywall can be converted into a soil additive.

It's Garbage, But Is It Art?

- Those of you with household members under the age of 20 already know about the hugely popular band that's a hit with the alternative rock crowd. The ensemble pride themselves on mixing as much pure noise and weird sounds as possible over their unforgettable musical prose. Clanking air conditioners, out-of-whack synthesizers and relentless blasts of unadulterated commotion are all fair game as they search for new and even stranger sounds to include in the type of rock they call "dark pop." Yes, it's true—a friend listened in on an early rehearsal and christened the band when he told them what they were doing was Garbage.

Paved With Good Intentions

- Pennsylvania Department of Transportation officials aren't answering any more questions about a little road-paving unpleasantness that made the news. Apparently, a deer that had been struck and killed on a state highway was overlooked when repair crews were refinishing the road, resulting in a large, deer-shaped lump of oil and stones in one lane of traffic. A department spokesperson said, "It should not have happened."

26

THE TITANIC

By Kathy Wolfe

First Fact

- The *Titanic* was built at a cost of nearly $8 million. James Cameron's 1997 movie *Titanic* was produced with a price tag of more than $200 million.

1912 Bits

- Nearly 14,000 laborers contributed to the construction of the *Titanic*.
- It took 44,000 pounds of soap, grease, and oil to slide the *Titanic* into the water the day she was launched.
- The *Titanic* was four city blocks long. The anchors alone had a total weight of 31 tons. The ship's weight was 46,329 tons.
- Three million rivets held the hull together.
- The ship required 650 tons of coal every day to feed its 159 furnaces.

In the Pantry

- The *Titanic* left Southampton, England with 75,000 pounds of fresh meat, 11,000 pounds of fresh fish, 36,000 oranges, and 40 tons of potatoes.
- The cooler of the ship contained 40,000 eggs, 6,000 pounds of butter, and 1,500 gallons of milk.
- 800 pounds of tea and 2,200 pounds of coffee waited to be served from the ship's 3,000 teacups and sweetened with five tons of sugar.
- 6,000 meals were served each day.
- The cupboards of the *Titanic* contained 12,000 dinner plates, 2,000 salt shakers, and 300 nutcrackers.

- 6,000 tablecloths and 45,000 napkins were on hand to set the dining room tables.
- The final evening meal served on the *Titanic* consisted of 11 different courses, including raw oysters as an hors d'oeuvre, cream of barley soup, cold asparagus vinaigrette, and roast duckling.
- Five grand pianos could be found aboard the ship.

Passenger Bits

- It was the plan of Captain Edward Smith to retire after navigating the *Titanic* safely to New York City. He had been employed for 38 years with the White Star Line, the ship's builder.
- J.P. Morgan, the richest man in America, cancelled his passage reservation on the *Titanic* at the last minute.
- The elegant first-class suites aboard the *Titanic* in 1912 varied in price from $3,500 to $4,350. This translates into $50,000 to $75,000 in today's money. Second-class passage could be had for $1,750 ($24,000 today), and third class was available for $30 ($345 today).
- The oldest passenger on the ship was 74 years old. The youngest was 2 months of age. The youngest survived the sinking, the oldest did not.
- The *Titanic* did not head straight for the Atlantic Ocean from Southampton, but first sailed 24 miles across the English Channel to Cherbourg, France, with a second stop for additional passengers at Queenstown, Ireland.
- Thirteen honeymooning couples went down with the *Titanic*.
- A male in third class had a one in 10 chance of surviving the disaster. The chances for survival for a female in first class were 9 in 10. Seventy-nine children were booked into third class, and only 27 survived.
- There were more than 2,200 passengers aboard the *Titanic* with lifeboat capacity for 1,178. As only 705 survived the tragedy, there was space on the lifeboats for nearly 500 more passengers.
- Although originally an additional row of lifeboats was to be

added to the deck of the ship, making a total of 32 lifeboats rather than 20, the management of the White Star Line scrapped the idea because they felt the deck would "look too cluttered."

Disaster Foretold?

- Morgan Robertson was a retired Navy officer who penned a novel about the most luxurious ocean liner ever built. He wrote of its maiden voyage from Southampton to New York and of how this "unsinkable" vessel struck an iceberg in the middle of the Atlantic. He detailed the shortage of lifeboats and the resulting deaths. Robertson christened his fictional ship *Titan*. Sounds like a chronicle of the ordeal of the *Titanic*, except that Robertson composed his prophetic novel in 1898, 14 years before the *Titanic* set sail.

April 15, 1912

- Icebergs are at their worst during the month of April, the month of the *Titanic* disaster. Warmer spring temperatures melt the thick ice of the sea that has held the icebergs in place, releasing them to float free.
- It would take 1,900 tons of dynamite to destroy an average-sized iceberg. Melting it would require the heat of burning almost 2.5 million tons of gasoline. It's estimated that the iceberg that the *Titanic* struck was 50 feet above water, with seven-eighths of its bulk below the water. Estimated weight of the iceberg is about 500,000 tons. Compare this with the ship's weight of 46,329 tons.
- The lookouts on the *Titanic* had no binoculars although they had asked for them several times. The crew member who sighted the iceberg claimed the ship could have been saved if the lookouts had been searching the waters using binoculars.
- Fredrick Fleet, the man who is said to have first spotted the fatal iceberg, survived the disaster, but committed suicide 53 years after the disaster.
- Based on the *Titanic's* speed, if the iceberg had been sighted only 30 seconds sooner, the collision could have been avoided.

- The wireless operators of the *Titanic* received seven telegraphed ice warnings the night of the disaster. The final message was placed under a paperweight and was never delivered.
- Captain Smith's final words to his crew were: "Men, you have done your full duty. You can do no more…now it's every man for himself."
- Although a lifeboat could hold 65 people, the first one was launched with only 28 on board.
- There was a sufficient number of lifebelts on the *Titanic*.
- Less than 20 miles from the *Titanic,* the *Californian* telegraphed iceberg warnings to the ship. They did not respond to the distress calls of the *Titanic*. The telegraph operator had turned off his wireless and gone to bed.
- The *Californian* also ignored the white distress rocket flares of the *Titanic*. They did attempt to signal the sinking ship with their electric Morse signal lantern, but gave it up when they did not receive a response.
- It took only two hours and 40 minutes for the *Titanic* to sink after she struck the iceberg. At the time of the impact, the ship was traveling at around 22 knots, the highest speed she had ever reached.

Discovery

- The wreck of the *Titanic* was discovered in September of 1985 approximately 400 miles off the coast of Newfoundland, 1,191 miles from New York, 12,460 feet below the surface of the North Atlantic. Robert Ballard led the expedition.
- During Ballard's 1986 expedition to the ocean floor, more than 20,000 photos were shot in four days.
- The bow and the stern of the wreckage lie 1,970 feet apart on the ocean floor.
- It was not a large gash in the hull of the *Titanic* that caused it to sink, but rather the force of impact that caused the steel rivets to pop, buckling the steel plates of the hull.
- Items that can be found in a Philadelphia *Titanic* museum include the lifebelt worn by Mrs. John Jacob Astor, a menu

from the dining room, a deck chair, and a piece of wood from a lifeboat.

- An early salvage proposal to "raise the Titanic" involved 180,000 tons of petroleum jelly packed into polyester bags. The idea was to place these bags inside the hull of the wrecked ship, and when the jelly hardened, the ship would float up. The ocean's incredible pressure of 6,000 pounds per inch prevents any "raising" efforts.

At the Movies

- It took Hollywood only one month to produce the first movie on the *Titanic* tragedy. The movie was entitled *Saved From The Titanic,* and starred an actress who had actually survived the disaster. It was released on May 14, 1912, exactly one month after the sinking of the ship. In the movie, actress Dorothy Gibson wore the actual dress she had worn aboard the *Titanic.*
- One of the officers who survived the sinking served as a technical adviser in the 1958 film *A Night To Remember.* When he died, his ashes were scattered over the North Atlantic in the vicinity of the *Titanic.*
- James Cameron made 12 trips, two miles under the ocean to the actual wreckage of the *Titanic* to research for his 1997 blockbuster film. His movie contains actual footage from his trips, shot on location.
- The wealthy character from Cameron's film, Caledon Hockley, was named for two small towns in Ontario, Canada, near the residence of James Cameron's aunt and uncle. The character of Rose was named after Cameron's grandmother.
- The 1997 *Titanic* had a cast of 150, 200 extras, and 800 crew members.

Titantic at the Movies

- The new car seen in the cargo hold of the ship in James Cameron's movie is a factual item. The William Carter family of America was bringing a brand new Renault back with them from England.

- The actors' icy, frozen hair in Cameron's movie was fabricated by coating hair with colored wax.
- Cameron's *Titanic* replica was constructed in Mexico City. It was sunk in a massive tank containing 17 million gallons of water. A hydraulic lift was used to tilt the tank and raise and lower the ship.
- The 17-million-gallon tank was carefully watched by 30 lifeguards at all times when filming was in process.
- A second smaller tank containing 5 million gallons of water was used by Cameron to film the shots of the destruction of the ship's interior. The full-sized set of the *Titanic's* interior was constructed over the tank.
- Lifeboat scenes were shot in yet another tank containing 350,000 gallons, where actors floated several hours a day.
- An 86-year-old actress portrayed the 101-year-old survivor of the disaster in Cameron's film. Today there are eight known *Titanic* survivors.
- Because many scenes of the 1997 film were shot in Mexico where the replica was built, the visual effects crew had to digitally install computer-animated puffs of breath coming from the actors' mouths as the actors supposedly stood on deck in the frigid temperatures of the North Atlantic.
- Since most *Titanic* victims froze to death rather than drowned, cast members of Cameron's movie were instructed on the stages of hypothermia in order to make their scenes more realistic. Cameron advised his cast, "It's supposedly a very peaceful feeling."
- One of the early jobs held by *Titanic* star Leo DiCaprio was that of acting in television commercials advertising Matchbox toy cars.
- "We've dressed in our best and are prepared to go down like gentlemen." – *Wealthy Entrepreneur Benjamin Guggenheim*
- The tombstone of a young Englishman buried in the Nova Scotia cemetery reads: "Each man stood at his post, While all the weaker ones went by, and showed once more to all the world, How Englishmen should die."

- One knot is equivalent to 1.516 miles per hour.

More April 15, 1912

- The ice field the *Titanic* encountered was 78 miles long.
- The *Carpathia,* 58 miles away, was the ship that responded immediately to the *Titanic's* distress calls. It carried 705 survivors into New York harbor where the ship was met by more than 40,000 people.
- About 330 bodies were recovered on a search effort in the North Atlantic during the days following the disaster. Of these, 150 were never claimed. Those unclaimed were buried in Halifax, Nova Scotia.
- Copies of the deck plans and passenger list of the *Titanic* can still be obtained. Actual chunks of coal from the wreckage can also be purchased.
- The name Wallace Hartley probably doesn't ring a bell; however, his violin music could be heard until the very last minute the *Titanic* was afloat.

Wallace Hartley played to the last minute

INDEX

C

The Tidbits® Paper:

The Tidbits® paper was first published by Steele Media, Inc., in Billings, Montana in 1993. In 1994 it started its successful expansion across the country and now appears in more than 100 areas. It is distributed not only to restaurants, but also to grocery stores, doctors offices, convenience stores, oil change centers, anywhere people have time on their hands. Publishers of the Tidbits® paper earn income by selling the advertising that borders the text. For information on how you can become a publisher of the Tidbits® paper, call Steele Media, Inc. at 1-800-523-3096.

Future Publications:

If you would like to be notified about future Tidbits® books and products contact Steele Media, Inc., P.O. Box 1255, Billings, MT 59103 (406) 248-9000 or 1-800-523-3096.